THREE POEMS

THREE POEMS

John Ashbery

THE ECCO PRESS
New York

First published in 1989 by The Ecco Press
26 West 17th Street, New York, NY 10011
Published simultaneously in Canada by
Penguin Books Canada Ltd., Ontario
Printed in the United States of America

LIBRARY OF CONGRESS CATALOGING-IN-PUBLICATION DATA
Ashbery, John
[Poems. Selections]
Three poems   John Ashbery.—1st ed.
p.   cm.—([American poetry series])
Contents: The new spirit—The system—The recital.
I. Title.   II. Series.
PS3501.S475A6   1989
811'.54—dc20   89-16867

ISBN 0-88001-227-7

10 9 8 7 6 5 4 3 2 1

for David

CONTENTS

THE NEW SPIRIT

I thought that if I could put it all down, that would be one way. And next the thought came to me that to leave all out would be another, and truer, way.

clean-washed sea

                              The flowers were.

These are examples of leaving out. But, forget as we will, something soon comes to stand in their place. Not the truth, perhaps, but—yourself. It is you who made this, therefore you are true. But the truth has passed on

                              to divide all.

Have I awakened? Or is this sleep again? Another form of
sleep? There is no profile in the massed days ahead. They
are impersonal as mountains whose tops are hidden in
cloud. The middle of the journey, before the sands are re-
versed: a place of ideal quiet.

You are my calm world. This is my happiness. To stand,
to go forward into it. The cost is enormous. Too much for
one life.

There are some old photographs which show the event. It
makes sense to stand there, passing. The people who are
there—few, against this side of the air. They made a sign,
were making a sign. Turning on yourself as a leaf, you miss
the third and last chance. They don't suffer the way peo-
ple do. True. But it is your last chance, this time, the last
chance to escape the ball

of contradictions, that is heavier than gravity bringing all
down to the level. And nothing be undone.

It is the law to think now. To think becomes the law, the
dream of young and old alike moving together where the
dark masses grow confused. We must drink the confusion,
sample that other, concerted, dark effort that pushes not to

the light, but toward a draft of dank, clammy air. We have broken through into the meaning of the tomb. But the act is still proposed, before us,

it needs pronouncing. To formulate oneself around this hollow, empty sphere . . . To be your breath as it is taken in and shoved out. Then, quietly, it would be as objects placed along the top of a wall: a battery jar, a rusted pulley, shapeless wooden boxes, an open can of axle grease, two lengths of pipe. . . . We see this moment from outside as within. There is no need to offer proof. It's funny. . . . The cold, external factors are inside us at last, growing in us for our improvement, asking nothing, not even a commemorative thought. And what about what was there before?

This is shaped in the new merging, like ancestral smiles, common memories, remembering just how the light stood on the water that time. But it is also something new. Outside, can't you hear it, the traffic, the trees, everything getting nearer. To end up with, inside each other, moving upward like penance. For the continual pilgrimage has not stopped. It is only that you are both moving at the same rate of speed and cannot apprehend the motion. Which carries you beyond, alarmingly fast out into the confusion where the river pours into the sea. That place that seems even farther from shore. . . .

There is nothing to be done, you must grow up, the outer rhythm more and more accelerate, past the ideal rhythm of the spheres that seemed to dictate you, that seemed the establishment of your seed and the conditions of its grow- ing, upward, someday into leaves and fruition and final sap. For it is to be transcended. . . . The pace is softening now, we can see why it had to be. Our older relatives told of this. It happened a long time ago but it had to happen, which is why we are here now telling about it. If you thought you received more than your share, you could tell about that too. It was a free forum where each one came to cast off these irksome memories, strip down for the night that had preceded us to this place. Surely this was, also, a time of doing, not harvesting, for nothing was ripe, noth- ing had then been planted. . . . An active time, tense at the forehead and nostrils before sleep, pushing into the near piles of sticks and leaves and being gently nudged by them in return. A segment, more, of reality. This must be remembered too, it is even very important, but will the memory call itself to the point of being? For it is more tired than anything else. And so it slips away, like the face on a deflated balloon, shifted into wrinkles, permanent and matter-of-fact, though a perversion of itself.

Because life is short
We must remember to keep asking it the same question
Until the repeated question and the same silence become
    answer
In words broken open and pressed to the mouth
And the last silence reveal the lining

Until at last this thing exist separately
At all levels of the landscape and in the sky
And in the people who timidly inhabit it
The locked name for which is open, to dust and to no
    thoughts
Even of dying, the fuzzy first thought that gets started in
    you and then there's no stopping it.
It is so much debris of living, and as such cannot be trans-
    mitted
Into another, usable substance, but is irreducible
From these glares and stony silences and sharp-elbowed
    protests.
But it is your landscape, the proof that you are there,
To deal with or be lost in
In which the silent changes might occur.

It's just beginning. Now it's started to work again. The vis-
itation, was it more or less over. No, it had not yet begun,
except as a preparatory dream which seemed to have the
rough texture of life, but which dwindled into starshine
like all the unwanted memories. There was no holding on
to it. But for that we ought to be glad, no one really
needed it, yet it was not utterly worthless, it taught us the
forms of this our present waking life, the manners of the
unreachable. And its judgments, though harmless and
playful, were yet the form of utterance by which judgment
shall come to be known. For we judge not, lest we be
judged, yet we are judged all the same, without noticing,
until one day we wake up a different color, the color of the
filter of the opinions and ideas everyone has ever enter-

tained about us. And in this form we must prepare, now, to try to live.

It is not easy at first. There are dark vacancies the light of the hunter's moon does little to attenuate. Ever thought about the moon, how well it fits what it has to light? And those lacquer blobs and rivers of daylight, shaken out of a canister—so unmanageable, so indigestible . . . Well, isn't that the point? No, but there comes a time when what is to be revealed actually conceals itself in casting off the mask of its identity, when the identity itself is revealed as another mask, and a lesser one, antecedent to that we had come to know and accept. You think of clean legends, of this waking as penetrating a solid block of day. But day is there to assure you that you can't have this in another way, as you could with the films and shadows of night, to tell you that your mutually amused half-acceptance is not the wrong way to start, at any rate, that any breathing is to be breathing into each other, and imperfect, like all apprehended things.

Nevertheless the winter wears on and death follows death. I've tried it, and know how the narrowing-down feeling conflicts with the feeling of life's coming to a point, not a climax but a point. At that point one must, yes, be selective, but not selective in one's choices if you see what I mean. Not choose this or that because it pleases, merely to assume the idea of choosing, so that some things can be left behind. It doesn't matter which ones. I could tell you about some of the things I've discarded but that wouldn't help you because you must choose your own, or rather not choose them but let them be inflicted on and off you. This is the point of the narrowing-down process. And gradually, as the air gets thinner as you climb a mountain, these things will stand forth in a relief all their own—the look of belonging. It is a marvelous job to do, and it is enough just to approximate it. Things will do the rest. Only then will the point of not having everything become apparent, and it will flash on you with such dexterity and such terribleness that you will wonder how you lived before—as though a valley hundreds of miles in length and full of orchards and all sorts of benevolent irregularities of landscape were suddenly to open at your feet, just as you told yourself you could not climb a step higher. This casual, poorly seen new environment (but how gladly you are aware of imperfect vision, this time!) is to be the new kind of arbitrariness for you, one that protects and promotes without ever leaving the time-inflicted lesions of the old, toward which you struggled so hard without knowing it. These are vanished with the saw-toothed anomalies of time itself, and an open, moist, impregnable order of the day—kind, generous and protective—surrounds you as the artless gestures of a beautiful girl surround her with nobility which may never be detected, the fountain of one's life. And one never need wish to see it, for its truth does not matter, and is unimaginable.

You were always a living
But a secret person

As much into life
Yet not wanting to "presume"
Was the insurance
That life churned thick in the after-feeling
And so, even more, a sign of what happens today,
The glad mess, the idea of striking out.

Such particulars you mouthed, all leading back into the
underlying question: was it you? Do these things between
people partake of themselves, or are they a subtler kind of
translucent matter carrying each to a compromise distance
painfully outside the rings of authority? For we never
knew, never knew what joined us together. Perhaps only a
congealing of closeness, deserving of no special notice. But
then the eyes directing out, living into their material and
in that way somehow making more substance than before,
and yet the outward languid motion, like girls hanging out
of windows . . . Is this something to be guessed at, though?
Can it be identified with some area in someone's mind?
The answer is yes, if it is experienced, and it has only to be
expected to be lived, suspended in the air all around us. As
I was going to say, this outward-hanging, ledge over the
pitfalls of mankind, proves that it is something you know,
not just as the tree is aware of its bark, but as something
left with you on consignment. And it need not just be, it
can grow, with you though not part of you, if you are will-
ing to see it as reverting back to nature and not as the ulti-
mate realization of Roman engineers, a stone T-square.

But how does this work? And yet you see yourself growing up around the other, posited life, afraid for its inertness and afraid for yourself, intimidated and defensive. And you lacerate yourself so as to say, These wounds are me. I cannot let you live your life this way, and at the same time I am slurped into it, falling on top of you and falling with you. At this point it is again time for forgetting, not casually so as to repeal it delightedly later on, but with a true generous instinct for ending it all. This is the only way in which new lives—not ours—can ever begin again. But the thought haunts me—will they be defined in terms of what we never were? Will the negative outlines of our never doing define their being, a repoussoir, and so enmesh themselves even more disastrously with their wanting to become? If that were the case it would be better to stop right here, in this room, only to continue breathing so that life might pursue its unwanted course, far from temptations of the future, yes that's it, so that in getting to know you I renounce any right to ulterior commemoration even in the unconscious dreams of those mythical and probably nonexistent beings of whose creation I shall never be aware. I'm sorry—in staring too long out over this elaborate view one begins to forget that one is looking inside, taking in the familiar interior which has always been there, reciting the only alphabet one knows. To escape in either direction is impossible outside the frost of a dream, and it is just this major enchantment that gave us life to begin with, life for each other. Therefore I hold you. But life holds us, and is unknowable.

They told this tale long ago
The legend of the children, in which they get closer
To the darkness, but go on living.
The motion of the story is moving though not
                                        getting nearer.

They told this throughout all times, in all cities. The
shape-filled foreground: what distractions for the imagina-
tion, incitements to the copyist, yet nobody has the leisure
to examine it closely. But the thinness behind, the vague
air: this captivates every spectator. All eyes are riveted to
its slowly unfolding expansiveness; it is the magnanimity
that creates this urge to emulate, like life, to grow, and it is
the shapeless modest tale, told in the cottage at twilight.
Progress to be born.

You know that emptiness that was the only way you could
express a thing? The awkwardness around what were nec-
essary topics of discussion, amounting to total silence on all
the most important issues? This was our way of doing.
Your body could formulate these things, projecting them
into me, as though I had thought of them. Everything
drops in before getting sorted out. This is our going now. I
as I seem to you, you as you are to me, an endless game in
which the abraded memories are replaced progressively by
the new empty-headed forms of greeting. Even as I say this

I seem to hear you and see you wishing me well, your eyes taking in some rapid lateral development

reading without comprehension

and always taken up on the reel of what is happening in the wings. Which becomes a medium through which we address one another, the independent life we were hoping to create. This is your eyes noting the passing of telephone poles and the tops of trees. A permanent medium in which we are lost, since becoming robs it of its potential. Nothing is to be learned, only avoided, nor can the truth of this be avoided, but it lingers on like microorganisms in the crevices. In you I fall apart, and outwardly am a single fragment, a puzzle to itself. But we must learn to live in others, no matter how abortive or unfriendly their cold, piecemeal renderings of us: they create us.

To you:

I could still put everything in and have it come out even, that is have it come out so you and I would be equal at the end of our lives, which would have been lived fully and without strain. But each of us has more of the vital elements than the other needs, or less: to sort them out would be almost impossible inasmuch as we are kept, each from the other: only the thawing nerve reveals it is time when one has broken out of some stupor or afternoon dream, and by then one is picking up for the evening, far from the famous task, close to the meaningless but real snippets that are today's doing. You understand we cannot casually borrow elements of each other so that it all comes out right. Force and mastery are required, they are ready in fact, but to use them deeply without excuses is a way of intermittent life, and the point was that the moments of awareness have to be continuous if they are to exist at all. Thus the sadness as I look out over all this and realize that I can never have any of it, even though I have it all as I in fact do. To be living, in each other, the perfect life but without happiness.

Well, this is what I get for all my plotting and precautions. But you, living free beyond me, are still to be reckoned into your own account of how it happens with you. I am afraid that you will never see your way clear through the velleities of the excursion to that other shore, eternal despite its finite nature, of acquisitions, suggestions and hints, useful, irregular: the exposed living that is going on, and of which you are a part, so that it could be said to exist only for you. You are too close to this happy state for it to matter for you. But meanwhile I am to include everything: the furniture of this room, everyday expressions, as well as my rarest thoughts and dreams, so that you may never become aware of the scattered nature of it, and meanwhile you *are* it all, and my efforts are really directed toward keeping myself attached, however dimly, to it as it rolls from view,

like a river which is never really there because of moving
on someplace. And so the denser moments of awareness
are yours, not the firm outline I believe to be mine and
which is probably a hoax as well: it contains nothing after
all, only a few notions of how life should be lived that are
unusable because too general. Nothing applies to your
strict handling of how the roots should be lived, without
caring about the flowers and leaves that may tower over
them, a subsidiary mass, someday. Only the day-to-day
implications matter for you. You are right, I suppose, but
there was this image as it once came to me, of its bright-
ness being together—not hanging together, for this implies
waiting to be seen—but existing as smoke up around the
bright levels of incidence and so on up into the sky, pu-
rified from being breathed in and alive from having lost
life at last. Leaving rolls of experience and they happen
further down too, are filling space up as they create more
space.

Is it correct for me to use you to demonstrate all this? Per-
haps what I am saying is that it is I the subject, recoiling
from you at ever-increasing speed just so as to be able to
say I exist in that safe vacuum I had managed to define
from my friends' disinterested turning away. As if I were
only a flower after all and not the map of the country in
which it grows. There is more to be said about this, I guess,
but it does not seem to alter anything that I am the specta-
tor, you what is apprehended, and as such we both have
our own satisfying reality, even each to the other, though
in the end it falls apart, falls to the ground and sinks in.

For I care nothing about apparitions, neither do you, scrutinizing the air only to ask, "Is it giving?" but not so dependent on the answer as not to have our hopes and dreams, our very personal idea of how to live and go on living. It does not matter, then,

but there always comes a time when the spectator needs reassurance, to be touched on the arm so he can be sure he is not dreaming.

We were just the other night leafing through some old declarations, nostalgic for the first crisp rendering of the difference, like an outcry, the difference between what separated us and what we were now going to do. How like children in the way of thinking that some beatific scrap may always fall and as time goes by and *nothing* ever happens one is not disappointed but secretly pleased and confirmed in one's superstition: the magic world really does exist. Its dumbness is the proof of this. Indeed any sign of activity on its part would be cause for alarm, since it does not need us, need to signal its clarion certainties into our abashed, timid, half-make-believe commerce of every day. So we grew up confident, in ourselves and in each other, confident that we would one day meet, strip ourselves of the real business of believing, preparing to live in the all-too-short night. And now these attitudes which were merely sketched on the air of the room have hardened into the official likeness of what we were doing there, the life has gone out of our acts and into the attitudes. So that we must despair of all realism now, because it is there, it is totally adequate for what was being represented, only we cannot feel it as such, but that is our tough luck. Indeed—is this really the end toward which everything was rotating? We wanted it to come out all right, and in the end that is what has happened. Others are sorry about other things. And we have the success of our gradual, growing belief in the importance of the universe as it came through to us to keep us going. Even the fact that there is no joy written into the ending, unless relief is the same thing, ought to be a comfort because it was recognized in the timid fairy-tale beginning that the happy ending was an artifice and that the happiness would be artificial, though real. Is it then that

we wanted the whole thing to misfire? to be caught off-base? or any of those myriad other expressions for failure that now come to mind? Is there something intrinsically satisfying about not having the object of one's wishes, about having miscalculated?

I can only say that the wind of the change as it has happened has numbed me, to the point where the false way and the true way are confounded, where there is no way or rather where everything is a way, none more suitable nor more accurate than the last, oblivion rapidly absorbing their outline like snow filling footprints. This despite the demonstrable rightness of the way we took, of our emergence into a reality that is perfect. Despite the satisfaction, endless as a sea.

You private person.

To every thing there is a season:
Today is cooler or warmer than yesterday, and it all works itself out into a map, projects, placed over the other real like a sheet of tracing paper, and these two simultaneously become what is going on. They can join, but never touch: such is the etiquette of knowing what you're doing, but they can get along in this way and progress can be noted. Your hair is fairer and your eyes are fairer. There can be no doubt you have outlived that early confusion and that now the outlines of a somewhat less perfunctory maturity have been laid down. Too, those other eyes and your fragmentary awareness of what they observed have tended to merge with your own as the focus was adjusted, and now the target—empty but with a rush of promise of fulfillment—lies under you, wonderful, the air you drink in in great gulps, laughing too.

It is not enough that these go hand in hand, what is wanted is some secret feeling of an administrator beyond the bounds of satisfying intimacy, a sort of intendant to whom the important tasks may be entrusted so as to leave you free for the very necessary task of idleness that is a condition, the condition, of your being, being together. This is not so easy. And already something like envy is lurking there, ready to destroy the whole solid but fragile mass with just a push too much. The whole structure must be subtracted from harm's way. It is better to take in a third person as a confidant, but since there is nothing to confide . . . But how much more prudent to have begun the whole thing in a different spirit, manfully, crossing each bridge as you came to it, flattening obstacles. . . . But there is no help for it and it must be remembered that the halfhearted, seemingly lazy way of moving forward is both the impetus and the nature of the work. It could have happened differently in no other world. And so tomorrow coming up is still a feast of expectation, is moving fast into the caves of your soul and this is the only way to have had the refreshment and the reward intact, in the midst of it all happening around you. There was no possibility of a bargain's being struck; it is offered this way and resumes its continuing in this way, in the clues to your personality. You have to take this as it opens up. There must be nothing resembling nostalgia for a past which in any case never existed. It is like standing up because you've been sitting all day and are tired of it.

However,
the honesty of this approach is eased, not softened, by its situation in the self-propagating wind. The wind is now fresh and full, with leaves and other things flying. And to release it from its condition of hardness you will have to take apart the notion of you so as to reconstruct it from an

intimate knowledge of its inner workings. How harmless and even helpful the painted wooden components of the Juggernaut look scattered around the yard, patiently waiting to be reassembled! So ends the first lesson: that the concave being, enfolding like air or spirit, does not dissolve when breathed upon but comes apart neatly, like a watch, and the parts may be stocked or stored, their potential does not leak away through inactivity but remains bright and firm, so that in a sense it is just as much *there* as if it were put back together again and even more so: with everything sorted and labeled you can keep an eye on it a lot better than if it were again free to assume protean shapes and senses, the genie once more let out of the bottle, and who can say where all these vacant premises should end? No, it is far better to keep this potential dry, even at the risk of having its immobility come to seem a reproach, the mute appeal of the saber hung up on the wall. If you don't start, you don't have to stop. But it is moving, though not moving satisfactorily, so that the reproach would be unjust. Why, its imperfections are just a token of how life moves along, haltingly but somehow always getting there in time, in our time. A cloak of somnolence, heavy and sticky as moonlight, translucent but imperfectly so (there are almost-transparent patches and parts that go under into darkness or some kind of unexplained activity—the whole is irregular, shifting, but up to its aim of clothing, concealing yet revealing) becomes the state of present affairs—one of erect passivity, polarized through hesitation and love, the odd details resolved but nesting in their quirkiness, free to come and go within a limited area, a sort of house-arrest of the free agent intentionally cut off

from the forces of renewal, obliged to spend a certain peni-
tential time of drawing in and not utilizing those intuitions
that gave wings, inspirations to fly abruptly out of the win-
dows of the house to the stars. If the truncated halves could
find each other again, and so on, and then the ideal parts
line up, their order into disorder, strong and vertical in the
spring night, the circuit could become perfect again. But
their unevenness is precisely the snag in the realization of
that perfect irregular order. They must disappear into
their odd angularity for a while, drift like the confetti they
are until the appropriate carnival mood opens and they
take fire like a haze of stars, ready to assume the light. In
this scheme of things what is merely pleasant has to die to
be born again as pleasure, and although it seems unfair
this includes your outside view, openness, your penetrabil-
ity and force to penetrate through outside agents that are
merely the logical extensions of your inner decision to act
and to bring this action to bear on the constellation of ev-
eryday phenomena. And so a new you takes shape. You
can stand it at first. If the beloved were an angel, then this
you would be the nameless spirit that watches from afar,
halfway between heaven's celestial light and dull Acheron.
But it is not necessary to sanctify the gods in order to live
in the suddenly vast surroundings that open out among
your features like pools of quicksilver: hours that seem like
minutes, invitations to spend time with strangers in un-
known places, no more disappointing orgasms, intentional
symbols, gestures a time's stand away, no more of the
group's reluctance to fully celebrate anything new. Yet
there is a narrowness too in this expansion that eternal
waiting slops over into, helplessly, in which you see your-

self as momentarily absorbed in some commonplace occu-
pation, but then the late afternoon gushes in to support
you, prop you up triumphantly in the narrow sector that
forethought and carelessness combined have brought you
to, monarch of all you survey and there is nothing mean or
squalid in being deprived, the space is aerated, and just as
the days get whittled down to more and more darkness at
the end of the year without one's wishing to be back at
midsummer, for this is somehow a higher ledge though a
narrower and bleaker one, so time running out does not
make this position less worthy or any of the individual in-
stants of light darker. As in a novel the unmistakable truth
of your character comes crashing through, having come to
mean what it had been called on for, and meanwhile the
tale itself, a bundle of incidents related to but separate and
distinct from you, got up and did a dance and left. If a
subconscious grievance persisted, a dream in which you try
to catch up to me in the street, still with the same features,
the glassy limpidity that both receives and projects the
aura in which we bloomed and later shriveled (how could
we know, any more than those insects whose life-span is a
single day?), it is there only because it is natural, because
"the public" expects it, to add in its own way a note of dig-
nity to this wholesome, tear-jerking ending that is both a
completion and the firm promise of a new beginning, first
the ball of string as the kite jerks it across the field and
then its shadow, fainter and fainter, with the idea of its all
being continued somewhere, in some more fortunate time
and place, but really: it's not a fairy tale, this time. It
wasn't so as to play real characters in an age-old fantasy
that we were combined: there is very little romanesque

element, more the ugliness of waiting and the obscenities
we think and speak, this is more like it, and somehow they
give dignity and immobility to us in relation to one an-
other. There are projections as we come to consider our-
selves, but no vulgar forced entry or forced turning away:
we remain separate forever, and this confers an admittedly
somewhat wistful beauty on the polarity that is our firm
contact and uneven stage of development at this moment
which threatens to be the last, unless the bottle with the
genie squealing inside be again miraculously stumbled on,
or a roc, its abrasive eye scouring the endless expanses of
the plateau, appear at first like a black dot in the distance
that little by little gets larger, beating its wings in purpose-
ful and level flight. I urge you one last time to reconsider.
You can feel the wind in the room, the curtains are mov-
ing in the draft and a door slowly closes. Think of what it
must be outside. Since time will in any case be reckoned
into the final addition, it is not as though you need con-
cern yourself. This is always taken care of. The whole
thing is calibrated according to time's way of walking side-
ways out of the event, at the same time proceeding in a
straight line toward an actual vanishing point. Already it
has moved us, toward and away from each other, farther
than we expected: the everyday glamor of a "personal
life," keeping a diary and so forth, is the outward sign of
this progression that is built into us like the chain of
breathing. So there is no need to wait to be transformed:
you are already. I am aware of it because I see you like a
star, that mild, friendly and warming presence so many
trillion miles away, and this suits me because I would have
you only in this way: as you are, as you are to me. There-

fore the major turn—third and last fateful step in the
triad, already moving into something else—cannot be
postponed, therefore there is no need to anticipate it, and
it would be impossible to do this. But I know that my rea-
soning falls on the ear like "special" pleading, it too is in
due season, and though all I really want to do is to call at-
tention to principles, it is part of growing up to accept this
new projection forward, and therefore we are to travel
abreast, twin riders dazzled and disintegrating under the
kaleidoscopic performance of the night sky this time, we
too projected sideways in advancing like waves pushed
away from the keel of a ship, rejoining in this way the se-
cret of the movement forward that made possible this full-
circle absorption of the voyage and its brilliant phe-
nomena—each distinct and, however modest, of a certain
importance in the hierarchy. Nevertheless storms do occur.
It would be inconceivable for the progression to pursue its
course unmolested, since it is a progression, for it not to be
narrowed down to that single moment of grabbing you
and shaking you mercilessly, nor that this moment become
the practical meaning of the pattern of events, thus to be
terminated "sadder and wiser," drawing the rueful lesson
from experience, and yet it was an accident, wasn't it? Not
just the part where everything went haywire but the whole
thing, a series of accidents complete in themselves and as
components fitting into one big accident? There would be
nothing very encouraging about this either except that our
shared apprehending of the course as plotted turns it into a
way, something like an old country road. We can stop, we
have stopped, we are stopping now, turning to look into
the fulfillment that each unconsciously exhibits to the

other, without wanting to especially or knowing too much about it. This possibility of fulfillment creates the appetite for itself, with the result that the dislocations come through to us as romantic episodes or chapters: "There's the one in which I fell away gradually, without even realizing it until we were already far apart, separated by new habits and preoccupations that had arisen even as we sat close to each other, talking about the weather and so on." To have the whole outline in mind yet not notice the individual changes as they occur, and then one day it dawns on you that you are the change, so naturally you could have seen it coming. A subtle corrosion has taken over this branching out, on a higher plane because the totality of its gradations had been breathed into the start, yet sinking deeper than that other that is cast aside because, whatever you might say of it, in the pattern of base voluptuousness it was perfect, a luminary, and things that are perfect of their kind are better than the flawed, interrupted spiral of that other narration whose purpose was to instruct and entertain, but which succeeded in doing neither because it was too turned in upon itself, and therefore suffered a shameful destiny, a chariot going down kicking and struggling at the first brush with the sun's deleterious rays. Quick thinking on your part saved us from such a melodramatic end, though: you merely restored the dimension of the exploratory dialogue, conducted in the general interest, and we resumed our roles of progressive thinkers and builders of the art of love. Not that such a thing could exist, or if it did it would certainly not be anything like an art, which can only exist by coming into existence, and then the rules may be drawn up, though it makes very little difference

since no one will ever play that game again. It lay there in
our already clouded vision as we looked at each other,
some dark beginning force that made it clear that the time
for action was past and the time for making speeches had
come. So, somewhat stimulated at the idea of not turning
back but going forward, making virtue of necessity, no
doubt, we proceeded to actually examine what there was
left for us. Not really, of course, but we could feel it as one
feels the temperature dropping even though one senses
only separate instances and not the movement of the fall.
It was waiting for us: the sense that we must now put our
ideas together and use them as steps for attaining some
kind of rational beauty within the limits of possibility, that
would not offend everyday experience, even of the coarsest
or most monotonous kind. A prison, in sum, but disguised
as a school, built on the false premise of education, that
the boredom now would necessarily result in some ulti-
mate note of improvement, though nothing resembling
that magnificent but empty structure we had started to
build incorrectly and had even begun to get used to de-
spite its having remained largely at the blueprint stage.
This was hell or worse, since there was no disproportion,
no juxtapositions to distract, nothing but the day-to-day
growth without change, no kind of manner in the sullen
sunlight that trickled in, illuminating everything equally:
a moral universe which the present had transcended but
which was able to reassert its authority during the confu-
sion that followed on its inevitable downfall and had now
emerged stronger than before: strong as iron. In the very
act of contemplating such a state of affairs prior to re-
jecting it one is caught up on the wheel, there is no alter-

native, and one finds oneself liking oneself and whatever it
is quite as much as ever, more in fact now that a sure sense
of purpose implements the drive into a definite thingness,
virtue still from necessity, mother of invention, but its own
reward. Remnants of the old atrocity subsist, but they are
converted into ingenious shifts in scenery, a sort of "Eng-
lish garden" effect, to give the required air of naturalness,
pathos and hope. Are you sad about something today? On
days like this the old flanking motion almost seems to be
possible again. Certainly the whiff of nostalgia in the air is
more than a hint, a glaring proof that the old irregular
way of doing is not only some piece of furniture of the
memory but is ours, if we had the initiative to use it. I have
lost mine. It has been replaced by a strange kind of happi-
ness within the limitations. The way is narrow but it is not
hard, it seems almost to propel or push one along. One
gets the narrowness into one's seeing, which also seems an
inducement to moving forward into what one has already
caught a glimpse of and which quickly becomes vision, in
the visionary sense, except that in place of the panorama
that used to be our customary setting and which we never
made much use of, a limited but infinitely free space has
established itself, useful as everyday life but transfigured so
that its signs of wear no longer appear as a reproach but as
indications of how beautiful a thing must have been to
have been so much prized, and its noble aspect which
must have been irksome before has now become inter-
esting, you are fascinated and keep on studying it. We
have broken through into the consequences of the grey,
sagging flesh that was our due, and it is surface enchant-
ment, healing to the eye and to the touch. But there is no

celebration of sensuality—there never could be, now—
only of its counterpart, a temporary dignity for the mind,
and waiting, that is satisfying anyway because it is a kind
of a way of being, any old kind but belonging to itself, in
and of itself and ourselves. The "luxury" of details that
coagulated into the old sad excitement told us so little,
really: at most the secret of choosing the most significant
ones to be put together into something to play that takes
up time, a scansion of that tough anxiety, ordering without
analyzing it. The rewards and punishments remain the
same, each accepted in a spirit of weary gratitude regard-
less of its nature. Take them away and the lived space will
not have altered, but will have drawn enough initiative
from the drop in tension produced by the sudden removal
of competition to expand its spark into a glow, suffusing
but not illuminating it, and the mind's suburbs too are
suddenly infected with the new spirit, commenting on it in
their accustomed lilting or droning vernacular; in some
cases it will take the form of clumsy removal of the barriers
by force—a slow but probably useful process; in others,
getting used to inhabiting the ruins and artfully adapting
them to present needs; in still others, standing up in the
space certain that it is the right one, and feeling the sense
of its proportions leave your mind like rays, striking out to
the antipodes and polishing them, perfecting them
through use. One can then go about one's business unen-
cumbered by nostalgia but still feeling the habit of this
place where one has accomplished things before; it will
change and you will go on thinking about it to your mu-
tual satisfaction and joy. The fact that you did all this—
cleared away all the debris so that the created vacuum

would expel you forward into an exact set of conditions replying to exact demands—fertilizes each instant as it is born, increases and dies, spontaneously generating the light that flushes through the silver-outlined mask of your face—baleful silver and black, the enchanter's colors—so that the lines gradually become invisible and disappear in the total modest radiance that builds up on its surface and finally blends with the ordinary daylight outside. And gradually the whirring and catcalls, rumbles and high-pitched screeches, the daily turnips and radishes, the *Kraut und Rüben* take over and are as if they had never ceased to be. I alone know that you were here before, even though nothing here any longer bears your imprint.

The problem becomes more definite. Smiling as though for the photographer, pleased to be here since it was promised you and has now made up for the lag in getting around to you, you overlap once again with the one that thought you, sent you speeding like an arrow into this pleasant desert where everything happens agreeably at a sign from you, in which you are still solitary despite the magnanimous currents in the air around you like a humming of wings. Safe, out in the open, and ready to start again,

only this time toward no special goal, its sense having become generalized in the environment, so that you are already part of it, a little, as you prepare to try to fathom its warpless and woofless subtleties. But it is hard, this not knowing which direction to take, only knowing that you are moving in one, not because no rest was decreed for you but because the force that shot you here remains through inertia, and even while contemplating the globe of seeming contradictions that grow out of your present standing you have begun to evolve in that other direction not included by the archer, a present time draped backward over the past, the appetites no longer chided, full in the expectation of becoming belief but just as surely periled by the negative of premature ripeness that haunts the joyous wilderness like the shadow of the grave.

At a sign from you these spirits could be set free from their tunnels in the earth to complete the circle of the act which you would have begun in this way, giving ideas to local deities of place and river gods to whom it might never have occurred otherwise that they might break open the one physical act they know and reveal the kernel like a picture that is taking place before them in order to proceed definitely into the future, sweeping aside all ifs and buts at the stately pace of a caravan disappearing into an undivided somewhere, all its secrets locked, swaying with the progressive movement toward and away from. But what is needed is some act other than pressing a button and having it all happen, some way of living into the layers as they occur and not losing momentum in order to strike,

except that in your night no knowledge can be present without your knowing it, and hence can never inflict itself on anything else. The various segments of knowledge are by definition divided up and distributed in an equilibrium guaranteed by the nature of their existence, yet it can all be grasped and used quite handily when an occasion presents itself. In among the trees that occasion may be growing, be ready to pounce on it holding the muzzle to its temple as the veins bulge, but there is a sickness built into this act of moving: it can never take place, only approach a buffer area where negotiations may be undertaken; in this way it prepares its own downfall while never quite beginning.

There is probably more than one way of proceeding but of course you want only the one way that is denied you, the leaves over that barrier will never turn the sorrowful agate hue of the rest but only burnish perpetually in a colorless, livid explosion that is a chant of praise for your having remained behind to think rather than act. Meditation rains down on you to be sucked up in turn by the sun like steam, making it all the more difficult to know where the branching out should occur. It is like approaching a river at night, uncertain of the direction of the current. But the pulsating of it leads to further certainties because, bouncing off the vortexes to be joined, the cyclical force succeeds in defining its negative outline. For the moment uncertainty is banished at the same time that growing is introduced almost surreptitiously, under the guise of an invitation to learn all about these multiple phenomena which are our being here, since a knowledge of them is after all vital to our survival in this place of provocative but baffling commonplace events.

What was it we said to each other? We must have spoken
to each other many times, but of these only the trace of the
words remains, and the expressions of your face and your
body

as you spoke or listened. Perhaps they are the most impor-
tant after all, like a writer's style. But now only the sound
of the truth as it is broken off from your mouth can kindle
this apathetic valley that wants nothing better than to
lapse back into the scenery of its dull vegetation. It wants
to surround, because this way you will accept yourself as
being here, in a place, any place, content to make the
rounds you know so well, the philosopher's daily walk that
the neighbors set their watches by.

You could then ignore the equal but opposed forces again
building up in you, though not forever since their paths
are not quite parallel and must eventually join in conflict,
a tormented sphere of cloud you carry in you like a blind
lantern. For the time being you can go on pretending that
it is enough to listen to those inner promptings, the voice of
the soul, until that fatal day when the look of the beloved
flashes on you with its intensity of fixed lightning. That
day you will realize that just having a soul was not
enough: you must yield it up, vanish into the oblivion pre-
pared for you by your years of waiting that all your prac-
tice of stoicism was not enough to seal off. And you know

at last the condition of weightlessness and everything it
implies: for the future, the present and most of all for the
past into which you now slip helplessly, no longer pre-
vented by the grid of everyday language, remaining in sus-
pension in that greenish aquarium light which is your new
element, compelled to re-enact the same scene in the old
park, with snow on the ground and the waiting look on the
faces of the nearest buildings, some distance away. All this
in the interests of getting at the truth.

Little by little
You are the mascot of that time
You have your own life too
But are circumscribed by the time's growing concern
So that your activities are diminished
Or simplified, like a dog's.

Yet it was almost enough to be growing up in that city.
The taste of it, rationed through a medicine dropper,
Filled up the day.
In the evening the newspaper was delivered, ready to be
     read.
Darkness glossed over the imbalances
And the last irregularities dissolved in sleep.
That metropolis was like the kitchen of the world
And we were like servants, setting out on the task of life
As on a tour of duty.

In summer our desires crossed
And were gradually veiled by foliage
Into a solid, bluish shadow
Yet one was aware of the living structure underneath
And sensed its pulsations at a distance
Imbibing the love as was meant
For it must be consumed
As surely as the appetite dies on the lips
And the guests move away in a chain.

So this meaning came to arise
Towering above the rest
With a place for each member of the family
And further up in the hierarchy
For every thought and feeling that had passed or would
    come to pass
In the finite universe defined by flocks of birds.
Simultaneously it was penetrable
And was being saturated by the direction of the journey
    we must take
Since it is before us helplessly waiting:
It must exist once the idea of it exists.
And so the meaning is brought down
To be with us together, never the same again.
We have passed through.

The aftermath of sunny days was a period so much like the
first, newly joined-together one that one might have mis-
taken it for part of an alternating pattern of planned

growth if the signal hadn't been given right away in the
form of a kind of fanfare of lucky accidents that drained
the succeeding weeks of any suspense. There could be no
doubt now that this continuing was merely another stone
added to the haphazard masonry of assorted beliefs that
was far from threatening to shut out the sun. And after-
ward as the calm illumination persisted one could even go
back to believing that this was the miracle, just as it had
been in the past. Oh, nothing so very miraculous, just a
feeling of being installed, as in a ship while it still rides at
anchor on the bay, of having been led to the starting point
and then proceeding a short distance, enough to erase any
serious doubts about the nature of the rest of the trajectory.
And yet it wasn't the same, since I was a very different
person by now and even recognized it. For starting out,
even just a very few steps, completely changes the nature
of the journey as it was when it lay intact and folded. That
first step ignites the endless cycle of rising and falling; it is
born; and one is aware of the still-invisible future as of a
sudden pause in the conversation that one could have pre-
dicted but didn't: sure enough, it's twenty minutes to the
hour or twenty minutes past, you say, and they all smile,
thinking obscurely of how this pause might have been
scheduled and where it has brought us. The days are get-
ting shorter, in fact quite a lot shorter. And suddenly you
have been occupied for some time with unlearning their
rhythm, drawing sleep about you like a blanket, but the
dotted rhythms persist and waking is somehow divided
up among them. You forget the salty and slightly bitter
taste of those morning dreams whose aim was both to mis-
lead and instruct. For a while they can be put away and it

is as though they disappear, and, faced with your satisfaction at being awake and free, you admit that there never was a day like this for getting things done, and action pursues its peaceful advance on the lethargic, malarial badlands of the day, draining swamps, clearing scrub forests, putting the hygienic torch to the villages, planting groundcover crops such as clover, alfalfa, colza, buckwheat and cowpeas. This is so. Yet there are other books, stories of how it might happen: merely to imagine them is enough to set one's head spinning, and swearing never to open any of them does no good of course, it sets the hydra in furious motion, pullulating beyond the limits of the imagination. But to have one person's affirmation of the way it happens for him . . . Yes, but you do not know this person.

He exists, but he is as a stranger for you in your own home. Just his being there beside you makes him a stranger because you can't tell how he got there. Nor can he, or at least he never seems to feel the urge to do so. So you are left with your blurred version slipping into mindlessness, but somehow merely being forced to focus on it brings it back, just for a while, but long enough to remind you that this happened before, and so on until a new occurrence important enough to eclipse all procedural questions and even to join you both in your singularity, reflecting each other's concerns for the first time and at the same moment seeing them vanish like Rumpelstiltskin, furious that you guessed the name.

At this point an event of such glamor and such radiance occurred that you forgot the name all over again. It could be compared to arriving in an unknown city at night, intoxicated by the strange lighting and the ambiguities of the streets. The person sitting next to you turned to you, her voice broke and a kind of golden exuberance flooded over you just as you were lifting your arm to the luggage rack. At once the weight of the other years and above all the weight of distinguishing among them slipped away. You found yourself not wanting to care. Everything was guaranteed, it always had been, there would be no future, no end, no development except this steady wavering like a breeze that gently lifted the tired curtains day had let fall. And all the possibilities of civilization, such as travel, study, gastronomy, sexual fulfillment—these no longer lay around on the cankered earth like reproaches, hideous in their reminder of what never could be, but were possibilities that had always existed, had been created just for both of us to bring us to the summit of the dark way we had been traveling without ever expecting to find it ending. Indeed, without them nothing could have happened. Which is why the intervening space now came to advance toward us separately, a wave of music which we were, unable to grasp it as it unfolded but living it. That space was transfigured as though by hundreds and hundreds of tiny points of light like flares seen from a distance, gradually merging into one wall of even radiance like the sum of all their possible positions, plotted by coordinates, yet open to the movements and suggestions of this new life of action without development, a fixed flame.

It was only much later that the qualities of the incandes-
cent period became apparent, and by then it had been
dead for many years. But in recalling itself it assumed its
first real life. That time was for living without the reflec-
tion that gives things and objects a certain relief, or
weight; one drank the rapture of unlived moments and it
blinded one to how it looked from outside, and—well, that
is what would have been necessary to give it the illusion of
duration that would have rounded out those other essen-
tial qualities and given them a reason to live for each
other. Otherwise their intensity evaporates from sheer
effervescence, leaving you pleasantly dazed and sleepy—
that feeling that comes after all great periods in history,
whose isolation is such that they seem to promise more
than even possibilities can give.

Behind this weather of indifference is of course a concern
for the real qualities that inform our continuing to see
each other about a lot of things. Luckily they are already
there, maybe they are what it is all about, though proba-
bly we tend to overesteem them because we had to dig
them out of the earth and clean them off and shine them
up. But they offer a pretext for looking into ourselves, ex-
amining the achievements of that easy time when an invis-
ible agency caused the meals to appear smoking hot on the
table, and afterward you could take home the gold and sil-
ver dishes on condition that everything next day would
have assumed its slightly guilty air of naturalness, for

sheepishness and a little feigned stumbling were always the note by which regular progression could be recognized and furthered in secret, and its achievements, through exercising those atrophied muscles of content and disbelief, had readied them for new accomplishments next to which those of the lunar phase would pale. It's true that a lot of grumbling had to accompany this and even an occasional bursting into tears, but that is the cost that reality, as opposed to naturalness, exacts. The wheels, constantly getting mired in the mud, have to presage a complete breakdown which must even occur over and over again in order to lead back to the quiet but superior normalities of life in eternity. What have we done? We cannot see through each other, the way is closed. Each has to go his own separate way, comforted only by the thought that it could never have been otherwise, and that this way as we understood it was the true one, leading to pitfalls of self-defiance and to our ultimate downfall as individuals with a concern for each other and for the welfare of the group.

The change is not complete.
The new morals have altered the original data
Which have again outstripped the message deduced from
   them.
The phenomena have not changed
But a new way of being seen convinces them they have.
We must live in the way of their gradually getting out of
   date
In order to plot the new change at the risk of predicting it
   this time.

Hence, diminished strength from paying too close atten-
tion to the curve of events,
Trying to imagine in advance what we were never in-
tended to know
Even as children, when knowledge was free.

And things decay into the pit left for them
By that greater happening as it is imagined:
Shorn of duration.
Just to be aware of the discrepancy isn't enough:
Knowledge does not make us happy.
It ought to be enough since
We sat to receive it
Passive and mutually shy
But this was the way we had chosen,
The way that leads to understanding.

Condemned to stand still
We now understood what had happened, not actively,
Which would have been to live again, but we understood
    it
As motionless, having no live projection
Beyond the fact of the words in which it was written down
And these took on special meanings,
Rigid, but beautiful, like a stained-glass window
As the light begins to improve and sharpen it
Until finally we had grown up in that region without ever
    having left it.

Still, it was possible to imagine everything that existed
elsewhere.

We were ideally happy. We had reached that stage in our
perennial evolution where holy thoughts no longer exist
and one can speak one's mind freely, and the night shot
back an answering fragrance: too far to the stars, but it
was here in its intimacy that wraps you in permissiveness,
leaving you free as it wanes to learn more about your spe-
cial thoughts or any ideas you might have. It is never too
late to mend. When one is in one's late thirties, ordinary
things—like a pebble or a glass of water—take on an ex-
pressive sheen. One wants to know more about them, and
one is in turn lived by them. Young people might not envy
this kind of situation, perhaps rightly so, yet there is now
interleaving the pages of suffering and indifference to
suffering a prismatic space that cannot be seen, merely felt
as the result of an angularity that must have existed from
earliest times and is only now succeeding in making its
presence felt through the mists of helpless acceptance of
everything else projected on our miserable, dank span of
days. One is aware of it as an open field of narrative possi-
bilities. Not in the edifying sense of the tales of the past
that we are still (however) chained to, but as stories that
tell only of themselves, so that one realizes one's self has
dwindled and now at last vanished in the diamond light of
pure speculation. Collar up, you are lighter than air. The
only slightly damaged bundle of receptive nerves is hum-
ming again, receiving the colorless emanations from outer

space and dispatching dense, precisely worded messages. There is room to move around in it, which is all that matters. The pain that drained the blood from your cheeks when you were young and turned you into a whitened specter before your time is converted back into a source of energy that peoples this new world of perceived phenomena with wonder. You wish you could shake hands with your lovers and enemies, forgive and love them, but they too are occupied as you are, though they greet you with friendly, half-distracted smiles and nods. The Hermit has passed on, slowly and haltingly, the light streaming from under his cloak, and in his place the Hanged Man points his toe at the stars, at ease at last in comfortably assuming that age-old attitude of sacrifice; the gold coins slither out of his pockets and fall to earth which they fertilize with many ideas, some harebrained, others daringly original. In the sky a note of fashionable melancholy has begun to prevail: it is the quick-witted devotion of Sagittarius, the healer, caustic but kind, sweeping away the cobwebs of intuitive idealism that still lingered here and there in pockets of darkness. The Archer takes careful aim, his arrow flies to the nearest card, the Five of Cups: "Trouble from a loved one. Trouble introduced into the midst of an already realized state. Amorous dangers. Perils through a woman." And also rectitude, for the aim was just. From the tiny trickle of blood from the wounded card a green stain grows; soon leaves shoot up and then tiny white odorless flowers, the promise of what still remains to be fulfilled. But of course since this was no shot in the dark it is an already realized state in its potential. The note is struck, the development of its resonances ready to snap into place. For the moment we know nothing more than this.

But the light continues to grow, the eternal disarray of sunrise, and one can now distinguish certain shapes such as haystacks and a clocktower. So it was true, everything was holding its breath because a surprise was on the way. It has already installed itself and begun to give orders: workmen are struggling to raise the main pole that supports the tent while over there others are watering the elephants, dressing down the horses; one is pretending to box with a tame bear. Everything is being lifted or locked into place all over the vast plain, without fuss or worry it slowly nears completion thanks to exceptional teamwork on the part of the crew of roustabouts and saltimbanques whose job this was anyway, and whose ardor need never have excited any jealousy on your part: they are being paid, after all. And one moves closer, drawn first by the aura of the spectacle, to come to examine the merit of its individual parts so as to enjoy even more connecting them up to the whole.

All this happened in April as the sun was entering the house of Aries, the Ram, the agent of Mars and fire and the first of the twelve signs of the Zodiac, bringing a spirit of reconciliation and amnesty amid the wars and horror that choked the earth; a feeling of sacrifice too and blood-

letting in the annual performance of the rites of spring.
The pure in heart rejoiced for they were sure now that
something terrific was going to happen. And as a matter of
fact in places all over the earth where the ephemeral sex-
ing was going on, the indifferent glances of adolescents
scarcely accosted their elders, who were themselves too
caught up in the excitement of the eternal tragedy to pay
much mind. The Ram is imbued with tremendous force
which can easily turn into shouted obscenities if he doesn't
get his way, as sometimes happens. He wants to go it
alone, but at this time of year the populations emerge
again into the arena of life after the death of winter, and
one is newly conscious of the multitudes that swarm past
one in the street; there is something of death here too in
the way they plunge past toward some unknown destina-
tion, leaving one a little shaken up on the edge of the side-
walk. Who are all these people? What does it mean that
there are so many? Is it possible that the desires of one
might not conflict with the desires of all the others, and
vice versa, or is it precisely this imbroglio of defeated de-
sires that is coming up now, a sort of Thirty Years' War of
the human will, terrible in its destructive surging that
threatens to completely annihilate the life which it so ebul-
liently manifests? One stays like this on the edge of the
throng, trying to think these things out. It may become
necessary to shut them all out, with the light of the sun
and the other planets, to retreat again into the hard, dark
recesses of yourself where you know no comfort is to be
found, but which are preferable nevertheless to this peril-
ous position on the edge of the flood, looking down awe-
struck into the coiling waters that sometimes strike out and

ensnare a parcel of land that had seemed secure. Surely there are things to be thought out, for the renewal of life poses terrible problems, no matter how fortunate in the context. At last there is the sense of destiny, the one thing that never could have happened, but even as its word fills your mouth you realize the terrible things that are left unsaid: what happens after that?

Something *is* happening. The new casualness had been introducing itself, casually of course, but suddenly its credentials lay everywhere. It was a new time of being born, looking ahead almost fiercely enough to be the ripe ear, and still keeping discreetly in the early stage of noncommittal promises. It wasn't the lily-pad stage yet, but there was buzzing everywhere as though the news had already broken out and was flooding the city and the whole country. The next day he rose up from that bed of reflective voluptuousness, determined never again to fall into the richly human excesses that his horizontal state had left him vulnerable to, having decided to grant a personal interview to each member of the enemy that blackened the plain as far as one could see in all directions. And the rumor strengthened with the night. In the morning they had all vanished at least as far as the nearest mountains and probably from the face of the earth.

Meanwhile he had taken the universal emotional crisis on his own shoulders, not from altruism but through a mistaken notion that things could be no other way, that riches would automatically result from the world's following its preordained course. And alas, to be releasing the prey for the shadow at this late date was, no doubt, to fall in with the plans of the cosmos, but how faintly it echoed, how pallid the evening glare that was supposed to strike fear into the hearts of nations! There was no getting around it, the Moon had triumphed easily once again, Hecate and her brood of snarling mutts were always around messing up the place, and in the meantime the crayfish had glided unnoticed out of the water and begun its upward course, drawn by some baffling magnetism toward its mother, the moon, who places everything in a false and puzzling light from which a fraction of the truth is not altogether absent, for the moon does illuminate, though erratically.

Thus summed up, he felt sickened at the wholeness. Better it should evaporate into the almost palpable clouds of the night than sit around as a reproach for all that was never going to be, now, since it included everything. Begone! But the solid block just sat there. Little by little its mass began to grow transparent, like clouds just before dawn. It was noticed that this transparency was the same as emptiness. There were no further alterations, none being necessary. Men went about their business as they had before, a little more disenchanted perhaps, but on the whole not un-happy; there was a lot of life to look forward to and a whole new assortment of celestial phenomena as well. But the one of whom this is written remained motionless. An-guish had pierced his soul, like the lead point of an arrow-head. Everything had stopped for him. There were no new

stories. Nobody invented things for him any more. He
tried to remember what it had been like before everything
had been canceled out, before the great Common Denomi-
nator had proved beyond the shadow of a doubt that
$ax^2 = ay^2$, but the difference between now and the other
hard times was that now there was no comfort in remem-
bering scenes of past unhappiness, indeed he was quite
sure there had never been any, and was therefore quite
content to remain as he had been, staring uncertainly into
the fire as though looking for a sign, a portent, but in real-
ity thinking of nothing at all.

It is very early.
The heavens only seem to be in a state of ferment.
If one might choose to see them differently there would be
Peace at the outer fringes
For their reluctance is never far away
And harmony, by the same token, is never ruled out com-
    pletely.

One can accomplish the thing quite quickly
And turn toward the ruled outside space
That defines our hesitations so majestically
Though negatively.

It is necessary to go forward completing
The gesture from the beginning of life
That was worrying its shape into the trees

All this time, as though that shape were responsible
For the many fluctuating situations that fill the air.

Ultimately only one continuous bell sound
Exemplifies the crowding around of
All the things that need getting done.
They fall away like memories of the seasons.

There is no staying here
Except a pause for breath on the peak
That night fences in
As though the spark might not be extinguished.

He thought he had never seen anything quite so beautiful
as that crystallization into a mountain of statistics: out of
the rapid movement to and fro that abraded individual
personalities into a channel of possibilities, remote from
each other and even remoter from the eye that tried to
contain them: out of that river of humanity comprised of
individuals each no better than he should be and doubtless
more solicitous of his own personal welfare than of the gen-
eral good, a tonal quality detached itself that partook of
the motley intense hues of the whole gathering but yet re-
mained itself, firm and all-inclusive, scrupulously fixed
equidistant between earth and heaven, as far above the
tallest point on the earth's surface as it was beneath the
lowest outcropping of cumulus in the cornflower-blue em-
pyrean. Thus everything and everybody were included

after all, and any thought that might ever be entertained
about them; the irritating drawbacks each possessed along
with certain good qualities were dissolved in the enthusi-
asm of the whole, yet individuality was not lost for all that,
but persisted in the definition of the urge to proceed higher
and further as well as in the counter-urge to amalgamate
into the broadest and widest kind of uniform continuum.
The effect was as magnificent as it was unexpected, not
even beyond his wildest dreams since he had never had
any, content as he had been to let the process reason itself
out. "You born today," he could not resist murmuring al-
though there was no one within earshot, "a life of incredu-
lity and magnanimity opens out around you, incredulity
at the greatness of your designs and magnanimity that
turns back to support these projects as they flag and fail, as
inevitably happens. But draw comfort meanwhile from the
fact that the planets have congregated to haruspicate at
your birth; they can no longer disentangle themselves but
are fixed over you, showering down material and immate-
rial advantages on whoever has the patience to remain im-
mobile for a while, mindless of the efforts of his coevals to
better themselves at the expense of humankind in gen-
eral." Nothing appeared to give ear to these rantings and
again light sank quickly into the low-lying mountains on
the horizon like water into pumice stone, as night again
erected with exact brilliance the very configurations he
had been invoking, so that it might have seemed a sar-
donic construction put upon his words to anyone who had
been there to notice. But the whole of mankind lay stu-
pefied in dreams of toil and drudgery; their miserable con-
dition offered no chance to glimpse how things were pro-

ceeding, no inkling that the fatal hour of liberation was advancing swiftly with measured and silent steps.

One day the thought occurred to him that it was still early, if you were to judge by how few events had actually taken place and how many others seemed to be waiting around half-prepared to come into existence if the demand arose. It wasn't that any of the previous forms of life he had taken: the animalistic one, the aristocratic one in which sex and knowledge fitted together to screen out the intriguing darkness, or the others in which idealism—child-love or sibling-love—gradually twisted the earth's barrenness into a sense from which both libertinage and liberty in its highest, most intellectual sense were subtly excluded, culminating in the (for him) highest form of love, which recognizes only its own generosity—it was not that these seemed no longer viable, stages in a progression whose end is still unseen and unimaginable. They had not merely served their purpose but were the purpose—what population is to the world, that explains as it uses it. But it dawned on him all of a sudden that there was another way, that this horrible vision of the completed Tower of Babel, flushed in the sunset as the last ceramic brick was triumphantly fitted into place, perfect in its vulgarity, an eternal reminder of the advantages of industry and cleverness—that the terror could be shut out—and really shut out—simply by turning one's back on it. As soon as it was not looked at it ceased to exist. In the other direction one saw the desert and drooping above it the constellations that had presided impassively over the building of the metaphor that seemed about to erase them from the skies. Yet they were in no way implicated in the success or the failure, depending on your viewpoint, of the project, as became clear the minute you caught sight of the Archer, languidly stretching his bow, aiming at a still higher and smaller portion of the heavens, no longer a figure of speech but an act, even if all the life had been temporarily drained out of it. It was obvious that a new journey would have to be undertaken, perhaps not the last but certainly an unavoidable one, into an area of an easier life, "where the lemons bloom," so that the last trials could be administered in an ambiance of relaxed understanding. You welcome these as an opportunity of definitively clearing your name, but are no less enthusiastic about the carefree, even frivolous atmosphere in which it all takes place—the sum total of all the good influences and friendly overtures in your direction, from which you have benefited intermittently all these years and which after periods of mutual discord have now banded together to create the impression of a climate in which nothing can go wrong, including the major question that revolves around you, your being here. And this is again affirmed in the stars: just their presence, mild and unquestioning, is proof that you have got to begin in the way of choosing some one of the forms of answering that question, since if they were not there the question would not exist to be answered, but only as a rhetorical question in the impassive grammar of cosmic unravelings of all kinds, to be proposed but never formulated.

THE SYSTEM

The system was breaking down. The one who had wandered alone past so many happenings and events began to feel, backing up along the primal vein that led to his center, the beginning of a hiccup that would, if left to gather, explode the center to the extremities of life, the suburbs through which one makes one's way to where the country is.

At this time of life whatever being there is is doing a lot of listening, as though to the feeling of the wind before it starts, and it slides down this anticipation of itself, already full-fledged, a lightning existence that has come into our own. The trees and the streets are there merely to divide it up, to prevent it from getting all over itself, from retreating into itself instead of logically unshuffling into this morning that had to be, of the day of temptation. It is with some playfulness that we actually sit down to the business of mastering the many pauses and the abrupt, sharp accretions of regular being in the clotted sphere of today's activities. As though this were just any old day. There is no need for setting out, to advertise one's destination. All the facts are here and it remains only to use them in the right combinations, but that building will be the size of today, the rooms habitable and leading into one another in a lasting sequence, eternal and of the greatest timeliness.

It is all that. But there was time for others, that were to have got under way, sequences that now can exist only in memory, for there were other times for them. Yet they really existed. For instance a jagged kind of mood that comes at the end of the day, lifting life into the truth of real pain for a few moments before subsiding in the usual irregular way, as things do. These were as much there as anything, things to be fumbled with, cringed before: dry churrings of no timbre, hysterical staccato passages that one cannot master or turn away from. These things led into life. Now they are gone but it remains, calm, lucid, but weightless, drifting above everything and everybody like a light in the sky, no more to be surmised, only remembered as so many things that remain at equal distances from us are remembered. The light drinks the dark and sinks down, not on top of us as we had expected but far, far from us in some other, unrelated sphere. This was not even the life that was going to happen to us.

It was different in those days, though. Men felt things differently and their reactions were different. It was all life, this truth, you forgot about it and it was there. No need to collect your thoughts at every moment before putting forth a hesitant feeler into the rank and file of their sensations: the truth was obstinately itself, so much so that it always seemed about to harden and shrink, to grow hard and dark and vanish into itself anxiously but stubbornly, but this was just the other side of the coin of its intense conviction. It really knew what it *was*. Meanwhile the life uncurled around it in calm waves, unimpressed by the severity and yet not paying much mind, also very much itself. It seemed as though innumerable transparent tissues hovered around these two entities and joined them in some way, and yet when one looked there was nothing special to be seen, only miles and miles of buoyancy, the way the mild blue sky of a summer afternoon seems to support a distant soaring bird. This was the outside reality. Inside there was like a bare room, or an alphabet, an alphabet of clemency. Now at last you knew what you were supposed to know. The words formed from it and the sentences formed from them were dry and clear, as though made of wood. There wasn't too much of any one thing. The feelings never wandered off into a private song or tried to present the procession of straightforward facts as something like a pageant: the gorgeous was still unknown. There was, however, a residue, a kind of fiction that developed parallel to the classic truths of daily life (as it was in that heroic but commonplace age) as they unfolded with the foreseeable majesty of a holocaust, an unfrightening one, and went unrecognized, drawing force and grandeur from this like the illegitimate offspring of a king. It is this "other tradition" which we propose to explore. The facts of history have been too well rehearsed (I'm speaking needless to say not of written history but the oral kind that goes on in you without your having to do anything about it) to require further elucidation here. But the other, unrelated happenings that form a kind of sequence of fantastic reflections as they succeed each other at a pace and according to an inner necessity of their own—these, I say, have hardly ever been looked at from a vantage point other than the historian's and an arcane historian's at that. The living aspect of these obscure phenomena has never to my knowledge been examined from a point of view like the painter's: in the round, bathed in a sufficient flow of overhead light, with "all its imperfections on its head" and yet without prejudice of the exaggerations either of the anathematist or the eulogist: quietly, in short, and I hope succinctly. Judged from this angle the whole affair will, I think, partake of and benefit from the enthusiasm not of the religious fanatic but of the average, open-minded, intelligent person who has never interested himself before in these matters either from not having had the leisure to do so or from ignorance of their existence.

From the outset it was apparent that someone had played a colossal trick on something. The switches had been tripped, as it were; the entire world or one's limited but accurate idea of it was bathed in glowing love, of a sort that need never have come into being but was now indispensable as air is to living creatures. It filled up the whole

universe, raising the temperature of all things. Not an
atom but did not feel obscurely compelled to set out in
search of a mate; not a living creature, no insect or rodent,
that didn't feel the obscure twitchings of dormant love,
that didn't ache to join in the universal turmoil and hulla-
baloo that fell over the earth, roiling the clear waters of the
reflective intellect, getting it into all kinds of messes that
could have been avoided if only, as Pascal says, we had the
sense to stay in our room, but the individual will condemns
this notion and sallies forth full of ardor and *hubris,* bent on
self-discovery in the guise of an attractive partner who is
the heaven-sent one, the convex one with whom he has had
the urge to mate all these seasons without realizing it.
Thus a state of positively sinful disquiet began to prevail
wherein men's eyes could be averted from the truth by the
passing of a romantic stranger whose perfume set in mo-
tion all kinds of idle and frivolous trains of thought leading
who knows where—to hell, most likely, or at very best to a
position of blankness and ill-conceived repose on the edge
of the flood, so that looking down into it one no longer saw
the comforting reflection of one's own face and felt secure
in the knowledge that, whatever the outcome, the struggle
was going on in the arena of one's own breast. The bases
for true reflective thinking had been annihilated by the
scourge, and at the same time there was the undeniable
fact of exaltation on many fronts, of a sense of holiness
growing up through the many kinds of passion like a tree
with branches bearing candelabra higher and higher up
until they almost vanish from sight and are confused with
the stars whose earthly avatars they are: the celestial
promise of delights to come in another world and still

lovely to look at in this one. Thus, in a half-baked kind of
way, this cosmic welter of attractions was coming to stand
for the real thing, which has to be colorless and featureless
if it is to be the true reflection of the primeval energy from
which it issued forth, once a salient force capable of assum-
ing the shape of any of the great impulses struggling to ac-
complish the universal task, but now bogged down in a
single aspect of these to the detriment of the others, which
begin to dwindle, jejeune, etiolated, as though not really
essential, as though someone had devised them for the
mere pleasure of complicating the already complicated
texture of the byways and torments through which we
have to stray, plagued by thorns, chased by wild beasts, as
though it were not commonly known from the beginning
that not one of these tendrils of the tree of humanity could
be bruised without endangering the whole vast waving
mass; that that gorgeous, motley organism would tumble
or die out unless each particle of its well-being were con-
served as preciously as the idea of the whole. For universal
love is as special an aspect as carnal love or any of the
other kinds: all forms of mental and spiritual activity must
be practiced and encouraged equally if the whole affair is
to prosper. There is no cutting corners where the life of the
soul is concerned, even if a too modest approximation of
the wish that caused it to begin to want to flower be the re-
sult—a result that could look like overpruning to the un-
trained eye. Thus it was that a kind of blight fell on these
early forms of going forth and being together, an anarchy
of the affections sprung from too much universal cohesion.

Yet so blind are we to the true nature of reality at any
given moment that this chaos—bathed, it is true, in the iri-
descent hues of the rainbow and clothed in an endless con-
fusion of fair and variegated forms which did their best to
stifle any burgeoning notions of the formlessness of the
whole, the muddle really as ugly as sin, which at every mo-
ment shone through the colored masses, bringing a telltale
finger squarely down on the addition line, beneath which
these self-important and self-convoluted shapes added dis-
concertingly up to zero—this chaos began to seem like the
normal way of being, so that some time later even very
sensitive and perceptive souls had been taken in: it was for
them life's rolling river, with its calm eddies and shallows
as well as its more swiftly moving parts and ahead of these
the rapids, with an awful roar somewhere in the distance;
and yet, or so it seemed to these more sensible than aver-
age folk, a certain amount of hardship has to be accepted
if we want the river-journey to continue; life cannot be a
series of totally pleasant events, and we must accept the
bad if we also wish the good; indeed a certain amount of
evil is necessary to set it in the proper relief: how could we
know the good without some experience of its opposite?
And so these souls took over and dictated to the obscurer
masses that follow in the wake of the discoverers. The way
was picturesque and even came to seem carefully thought
out; controls were waiting, in case things got out of hand,
to restore the inevitable balance of happiness and woe;
meanwhile the latter kept gradually diminishing whenever
its turn came round and one really felt that one had set
one's foot on the upward path, the spiral leading from the
motley darkened and lightened landscape here below to

the transparent veils of heaven. All that was necessary were patience and humbleness in recognizing one's errors, so as to be sure of starting out from the right place the next time, and so a sense of steady advancement came to reward one's efforts each time it seemed that one had been traveling too long without a view of the sun. And even in darkest night this sense of advancement came to whisper at one's side like a fellow traveler pointing the way.

Things had endured this way for some time, so that it began to seem as though some permanent way of life had installed itself, a stability immune to the fluctuations of other eras: the pendulum that throughout eternity has swung successively toward joy and grief had been stilled by a magic hand. Thus for the first time it seemed possible to consider ways toward a more fruitful and harmonious manner of living, without the fear of an adverse fate's coming to reduce one's efforts to nothing so soon as undertaken. And yet it seemed to those living as though even this state had endured for a considerable length of time. No one had anything against it, and most reveled in the creative possibilities its freedom offered, yet to all it seemed as though a major development had been holding off for quite a while and that its effects were on the verge of being felt, if only the present could give a slight push into the haphazard field of potentiality that lay stretched all around like a meadow full of wild flowers whose delightful promise lies so apparent that all question of entry into it and enjoyment is suspended for the moment. Hence certain younger spectators felt that all had already come to an end, that the progress toward infinity had crystallized in them, that they in fact were the other they had been awaiting, and that any look outward over the mild shoals of possibilities that lay strewn about as far as the eye could see was as gazing into a mirror reflecting the innermost depths of the soul.

Who has seen the wind? Yet it was precisely this that these enterprising but deluded young people were asking themselves. They were correct in assuming that the whole question of behavior in life has to be rethought each second; that not a breath can be drawn nor a footstep taken without our being forced in some way to reassess the age-old problem of what we are to do here and how did we get here, taking into account our relations with those about us and with ourselves, and the ever-present issue of our eternal salvation, which looms larger at every moment—even when forgotten it seems to grow like the outline of a mountain as one approaches it. To be always conscious of these multiple facets is to incarnate a dimensionless organism like the wind's, a living concern that can know no rest, by definition: it *is* restlessness. But this condition of eternal vigilance had been accepted with the understanding that somehow it would also mirror the peace that all awaited so impatiently: it could not proceed unless the generalized shape of this nirvana-like state could impose its form on the continually active atoms of the moving forward which was the price it exacted: hence a dilemma for any but the unrepentant hedonists or on the contrary those who chose to remain all day on the dung-heap, rending their hair and clothing and speaking of sackcloth and ashes: these, by far the noisiest group, made the least impression as usual, yet the very fact that they existed pointed to what seemed to be a tragic flaw in the system's structure; for among penance or perpetual feasting or the draconian requirements of a conscience eternally mobilized against itself, feeding on itself in order to re-create itself in a shape that the next instant would destroy, how was one to choose? So that those who assumed that they had reached the end of an elaborate but basically simple progression, the logical last step of history, came more and more to be the dominant party: a motley group but with many level heads among them, whose voices chanting the wise maxims of regular power gradually approached the point of submerging the other cacophony of tinkling cymbals and wailing and individual voices raised in solemn but unreal debate. This was the logical cutting-off place, then: ahead might lie new forms of life, some of them beautiful perhaps, but the point was that the effort of establishing them or anything else that was to come had ended here: a permanent now had taken over and was free to recast the old forms, riddles that had been expected to last until the Day of Judgment, as it saw fit, in whatever shape seemed expedient for living the next few crucial moments into a future without controls.

It seemed, just for a moment, that a new point had now been reached. It was not the time for digressions yet it made them inevitable, like a curtain at the end of an act. It brought you to a pass where turning back was unthinkable, and where further progress was possible only after it had been discussed at length, but which also outlawed discussion. Life became a pregnant silence, but it was understood that the silence was to lead nowhere. It became impossible to breathe easily in this constricted atmosphere. We ate little, for it seemed that in this way we could produce the inner emptiness from which alone understanding can spring up, the tree of contradictions, joyous and living, investing that hollow void with its complicated material self. At this time we were surrounded by old things, such as need not be questioned but which distill the meek information that is within them like a perfume on the air, to be used and disposed of; and also by certain new things which wear their newness like a quality, perhaps as an endorsement of the present, in all events as a vote of confidence in the currency of the just-created as a common language available to all men of good will, however disturbing the times themselves might turn out to be. Gradually one grew less aware of the idea of not turning back imposed as a condition for progress, as one imbibed the magic present that drew everything—the old and the new—along in the net of its infectious charm. Surely it would be possible to profit from the options of this cooperative new climate as though they were a charter instead of a vague sense of well-being, like a mild day in early spring, ready to be dashed to pieces by the first seasonable drop in temperature. And meanwhile there was a great sense of each one's going about his business, quiet in the elation of that accomplishment, as though it were enough to set one's foot on a certain path to be guaranteed of arriving at some destination. Yet the destinations were few. What actually was *wanted* from this constructive feeling? A "house by the side of the road" in which one could stay indefinitely, arranging new opportunities and fixing up old ones so that they mingled in a harmonious mass that could be called living with a sense of purpose? No, what was wanted and was precisely lacking in this gay and salubrious desert was an end to the "end" theory whereby each man was both an idol and the humblest of idolaters, in other words the antipodes of his own universe, his own redemption or his own damnation, with the rest of the world as a painted backdrop to his own monodrama of becoming of which he was the lone impassioned spectator. But the world avenges itself on those who would lose it by skipping over the due process of elimination, from whatever altruistic motive, by incrusting itself so thoroughly in these efforts at self-renewal that no amount of wriggling can dislodge its positive or negative image from all that is contemplated of present potentialities or the great sane simplifications to come. So that it was all lost, or rather all in the shade that instills weariness and sickness into the limbs under the guise of enraptured satiety. There was, again, no place to go, that is, no place that would not make a mockery of the place already left, casting all progress forward into the confusion of an eternally misapplied present. This was the stage to which reason and intuition working so well together had brought us, but it was scarcely their fault if now fear at the longest shadows of approaching darkness began to prompt thoughts of stopping somewhere for the night, as well as a serious doubt that any such place existed on the face of the earth.

On this Sunday which is also the last day of January let us pause for a moment to take note of where we are. A new year has just begun and now a new month is coming up, charged with its weight of promise and probable disappointments, standing in the wings like an actor who is conscious of nothing but the anticipated cue, totally absorbed, a pillar of waiting. And now there is no help for it but to be cast adrift in the new month. One is plucked from one month to the next; the year is like a fast-moving Ferris wheel; tomorrow all the riders will be under the sign of February and there is no appeal, one will have to get used to living with its qualities and perhaps one will even adjust to them successfully before the next month arrives with a whole string of new implications in its wake. Just to live this way is impossibly difficult, but the strange thing is that no one seems to notice it; people sail along quite comfortably and actually seem to enjoy the way the year progresses, and they manage to fill its widening space with multiple activities which apparently mean a lot to them. Of course some are sadder than the others but it doesn't seem to be because of the dictatorship of the months and years, and it goes away after a while. But the few who want order in their lives and a sense of growing and progression toward a fixed end suffer terribly. Sometimes they try to dope their consciousness of the shifting but ineluctable grid of time that has been arbitrarily imposed on them with alcohol or drugs, but these lead merely to mornings after whose waking is ten times more painful than before, bringing with it a new and more terrible realization of the impossibility of reconciling their own ends with those of the cosmos. If by chance you should be diverted or distracted for a moment

from awareness of your imprisonment by some pleasant or
interesting occurrence, there is always the shape of the in-
dividual day to remind you. It is a microcosm of man's life
as it gently wanes, its long morning shadows getting
shorter with the approach of noon, the high point of the
day which could be likened to that sudden tremendous
moment of intuition that comes only once in a lifetime,
and then the fuller, more rounded shapes of early after-
noon as the sun imperceptibly sinks in the sky and the
shadows start to lengthen, until all are blotted in the steal-
thy coming of twilight, merciful in one sense that it hides
the differences, blemishes as well as beauty marks, that
gave the day its character and in so doing caused it to be
another day in our limited span of days, the reminder that
time is moving on and we are getting older, not older
enough to make any difference on this particular occasion,
but older all the same. Even now the sun is dropping
below the horizon; a few moments ago it was still light
enough to read but now it is no more, the printed charac-
ters swarm over the page to create an impressionistic blur.
Soon the page itself will be invisible. Yet one has no urge
to get up and put on a light; it is enough to be sitting here,
grateful for the reminder that yet another day has come
and gone, and you have done nothing about it. What
about the morning resolutions to convert all the confused
details in the air about you into a column of intelligible
figures? To draw up a balance sheet? This naturally went
undone, and you are perhaps grateful also for your lazi-
ness, glad that it has brought you to this pass where you
must now face up to the day's inexorable end as indeed we
must all face up to death some day, and put our faith in

some superior power which will carry us beyond into a region of light and timelessness. Even if we had done the things we ought to have done it probably wouldn't have mattered anyway as everyone always leaves something undone and this can be just as ruinous as a whole life of crime or dissipation. Yes, in the long run there is something to be said for these shiftless days, each distilling its drop of poison until the cup is full; there is something to be said for them because there is no escaping them.

On the streets, in private places, they have no idea of the importance of these things. This exists only in our own minds, that is not in any place, nowhere. Possibly then it does not exist. Even its details are hazardous to consider. Most people would not consider it in its details, because (a) they would argue that details, no matter how complete, can give no adequate idea of the whole, and (b), because the details can too easily become fetishes, i.e., become prized for themselves, with no notion of the whole of which they were a part, with only an idolatrous understanding of the qualities of the particular detail. Certainly even this limited understanding can lead to a conception of beauty, insofar as any detail is a microcosm of the whole, as is so often the case. Thus you find people whose perfect understanding of love is deduced from lust, as the description of a flower can generate an idea of what it looks like. It is even possible that this irregular but satisfying understanding is the only one really allotted to us; that knowledge of the whole is impossible or at least so impractical as to be rarely or never feasible; that as we are born among imper-

fections we are indeed obligated to use them toward an as-
similation of the imperfections that we are and the greater
ones that we are to become; that not to do so would be to
sin against nature, that is to end up with nothing, not even
the reassuring knowledge that we have sinned to some
purpose, but are instead empty and blameless as an inani-
mate object. Yet we know not what we are to become,
therefore we can never completely rule out the possibility
of intellectual understanding, even though it seems noth-
ing but a snare and a delusion; we might miss out on ev-
erything by ignoring its call to order, which is in fact audi-
ble to each of us; therefore how can we decide? It is no
solution either to combine the two approaches, to borrow
from right reason or sensory data as the case seems to war-
rant, for an amalgam is not completeness either, and in-
deed is far less likely to be so through an error in dosage.
So of the three methods: reason, sense, or a knowing com-
bination of both, the last seems the least like a winner, the
second problematic; only the first has some slim chance of
succeeding through sheer perversity, which is possibly the
only way to succeed at all. Thus we may be spared at least
the agonizing wading through a slew of details of theories
of action at the risk of getting hopelessly bogged down in
them: better the erratic approach, which wins all or at
least loses nothing, than the cautious semifailure; better
Don Quixote and his windmills than all the Sancho Pan-
zas in the world; and may it not eventually turn out that
to risk all is to win all, even at the expense of intimate, vis-
ceral knowledge of the truth, of its graininess and contours,
even though this approach leads despite its physicality to
no practical understanding of the truth, no grasp of how to

use it toward ends it never dreams of? This, then, is surely
the way; but discovery of where it begins is another mat-
ter.

The great careers are like that: a slow burst that narrows
to a final release, pointed but not acute, a life of suffering
redeemed and annihilated at the end, and for what? For a
casual moment of knowing that is here one minute and
gone the next, almost before you were aware of it? Whole
tribes of seekers of phenomena who mattered very much to
themselves have gone up in smoke in the space of a few
seconds, with less fuss than a shooting star. Is it then that
our bodies combined in such a way as to show others that
we really mean it to each other—is this really all we ever
intended to do? Having been born with knowledge or at
least with the capacity to judge, to spend all our time
working toward a way to show off that knowledge, so as to
be able to return to it at the end for what it is? Besides the
obvious question of who knows whether it will still be
there, there is the even more urgent one of whose life are
we taking into our hands? Is there no way in which these
things may be done for themselves, so that others may
enjoy them? Already we have wandered far from the track
and, as always happens in such cases, darkness has fallen
and it would be impossible to find one's way back without
getting lost. Is this a reason to stay where we are, on the
false assumption that we are less lost right here, and thus
to complete the cycle of inertia that we began wrongly
supposing that it would lead to knowledge? No, it is far
better to continue on our way, even at the risk of getting

more lost (an impossibility, of course). We might at least wind up with a knowledge of who *they* are, with whom we began, and at the very least with a new respect toward the others, reached through a more perfect understanding of ourselves and the true way. But still the "career" notion intervenes. It is impossible for us at the present time not to think of these people as separate entities, each with his development and aim to be achieved, careers which will "peak" after a while and then go back to being ordinary lives that fade quite naturally into air as they are used up, and are as though they never were, except for the "lesson" which has added an iota to the sum of all human understanding. And this way of speaking has trapped each one of us.

An alternative way would be the "life-as-ritual" concept. According to this theory no looking back is possible, in itself a considerable advantage, and the stages of the ritual are each considered in themselves, for themselves, but here no danger of fetishism is possible because all contact with the past has been severed. Fetishism comes into being only when there is a past that may seem more or less attractive when compared with the present; the resulting inequality causes a rush toward the immediate object of contemplation, hardens it into a husk around its own being, which promptly ceases. But the ritual approach provides some bad moments too. All its links severed with the worldly matrix from which it sprang, the soul feels that it is propelling itself forward at an ever-increasing speed. This very speed becomes a source of intoxication and of more

gradually accruing speed; in the end the soul cannot rec-
ognize itself and is as one lost, though it imagines it has
found eternal rest. But the true harmony which would ren-
der this peace interesting is lacking. There is only a cold
knowledge of goodness and nakedness radiating out in
every direction like the spines of the horse chestnut; mere
knowledge and experience without the visual irregulari-
ties, those celestial motes in the eye that alone can trans-
form ecstasy into a particular state beyond the dearly won
generality. Here again, if backward looks were possible,
not nostalgia but a series of carefully selected views, hier-
atic as icons, the difficulty would be eased and self could
merge with selflessness, in a true appreciation of the tre-
mendous volumes of eternity. But this is impossible be-
cause the ritual is by definition something impersonal, and
can only move further in that direction. It was born with-
out a knowledge of the past. And any attempt to hybridize
it can only result in destruction and even death.

In addition to these twin notions of growth, two kinds of
happiness are possible: the frontal and the latent. The first
occurs naturally throughout life; it is experienced as a
kind of sense of immediacy, even urgency; often we first
become aware of it at a moment when we feel we need
outside help. Its sudden balm suffuses the soul without
warning, as a kind of bloom or grace. We suppose that
souls "in glory" feel this way permanently, as a day-to-day
condition of being: yes, as a condition, for it is both more
and less than a state; it exacts certain prerequisites and
then it builds on these, but the foundation is never forgot-

ten; it is the foundation that is happiness. And as it exacts, so it bestows. There is not the mindlessness, no idea of eternal lassitude permeated with the light of the firmament or whatever; there are only the value judgments of truth, exposed one after another like colored slides on the white wall that is the naked soul, or a kind of hard glaze that definitively transforms the ordinary clay of the soul into an object of beauty by obliterating the knowledge of what lies underneath. This is what we are all hoping for, yet we know that very few among us will ever achieve it; those who do will succeed less through their own efforts than through the obscure workings of grace as chance, so that although we would be very glad to have the experience of this sudden opening up, this inundation which shall last an eternity, we do not bother our heads too much about it, so distant and far away it seems, like those beautiful mosaic ceilings representing heaven which we crane up at from below, knowing that we cannot get near enough for it to be legible but liking all the same the vastness and aura of the conception, glad to have seen it and to know it's there but nevertheless firmly passing outward into the sunlight after two or three turns around the majestic dim interior. This kind of beauty is almost too abstract to be experienced as beauty, and yet we must realize that it is not an abstract notion, that it really can happen at times and that life at these times seems marvelous. Indeed this is truly what we were brought into creation for, if not to experience it, at least to have the knowledge of it as an ideal toward which the whole universe tends and which therefore confers a shape on the random movements outside us—these are all straining in the same direction, toward the

same goal, though it is certain that few if any of those we
see now will attain it.

The second kind, the latent or dormant kind, is harder to
understand. We all know those periods of balmy weather
in early spring, sometimes even before spring has officially
begun: days or even a few hours when the air seems
suffused with an unearthly tenderness, as though love were
about to start, now, at this moment, on an endless journey
put off since the beginning of time. Just to walk a few steps
in this romantic atmosphere is to experience a magical but
quiescent bliss, as though the torch of life were about to be
placed in one's hands: after having anticipated it for so
long, what is one now to do? And so the happiness with-
holds itself, perhaps even indefinitely; it realizes that the
vessel has not yet been fully prepared to receive it; it is
afraid it will destroy the order of things by precipitating it-
self too soon. But this in turn quickens the dismay of the
vessel or recipient; it, or we, have been waiting all our lives
for this sign of fulfillment, now to be abruptly snatched
away so soon as barely perceived. And a kind of panic de-
velops, which for many becomes a permanent state of
being, with all the appearances of a calm, purposeful,
reflective life. These people are awaiting the sign of their
felicity without hope; its *nearness* is there, tingeing the air
around them, in suspension, in escrow as it were, but they
cannot get at it. Yet so great is their eagerness that they
believe that they have already absorbed it, that they have
attained that plane of final realization which we are all
striving for, that they have achieved a state of permanent

grace. Hence the air of joyful resignation, the beatific up-
turned eyelids, the paralyzed stance of these castaways of
the eternal voyage, who imagine they have reached the
promised land when in reality the ship is sinking under
them. The great fright has turned their gaze upward, to
the stars, to the heavens; they see nothing of the disarray
around them, their ears are closed to the cries of their fel-
low passengers; they can think only of themselves when all
the time they believe that they are thinking of nothing but
God. Yet in their innermost minds they know too that all
is not well; that if it were there would not be this rigidity,
with the eye and the mind focused on a nonexistent center,
a fixed point, when the common sense of even an idiot
would be enough to make him realize that nothing has
stopped, that we and everything around us are moving for-
ward continually, and that we are being modified con-
stantly by the speed at which we travel and the regions
through which we pass, so that merely to think of ourselves
as having arrived at some final resting place is a contradic-
tion of fundamental logic, since even the dullest of us
knows enough to realize that he is ignorant of everything,
including the basic issue of whether we are in fact moving
at all or whether the concept of motion is something that
can even be spoken of in connection with such ignorant
beings as we, for whom the term ignorant is indeed per-
haps an overstatement, implying as it does that something
is known somewhere, whereas in reality we are not even
sure of this: we in fact cannot aver with any degree of cer-
tainty that we *are* ignorant. Yet this is not so bad; we have
at any rate kept our open-mindedness—*that,* at least, we
may be sure that we have—and are not in any danger, or

so it seems, of freezing into the pious attitudes of those true spiritual bigots whose faces are turned toward eternity and who therefore can see nothing. We know that we are en route in a certain sense, and also that there has been a hitch somewhere: we have as it were boarded the train but for some unexplained reason it has not yet started. But there is in this as yet only slight delay matter for concern even for the likes of us, intelligent and only modestly expectant as we are, patient, meek without any overtones of ironic resignation before a situation we are powerless to change and secretly believe is likely to go from bad to worse. There is nothing of that in us, we are not bigots and we have kept an open mind, we have all our mobility in a word, yet we too sense a danger and we do not quite know how we are going to react. Those first few steps, in the prematurely mild air that a blizzard is surely destined to dash from living memory before tomorrow comes—aren't we in danger of accepting these only for what they are, of being thankful for them and letting our gratitude take the place of further inquiry into what they were like, of letting it stand both for our attitude as eternity will view it and also for the fulfillment of which this was just the promise? That surely is the danger we run in our state of sophisticated but innocent enlightenment: that of not *demanding* and getting a hearing, of not finding out where these steps were leading even in the teeth of an almost dead certainty that it was nowhere, even of doubting that they ever took place, that any kind of structure or fabric in which they would assume being could ever have existed. So that in our way we are worse off or at least in worse danger than those others who imagine themselves already delivered from the chain of rebirth. *They* have their illusions to sustain them, even though these are full of holes and sometimes don't prevent their possessors from feeling the chilly drafts of doubt, while we can be brought to doubt that any of this, which we know in our heart of hearts to be a real thing, an event of the highest spiritual magnitude, ever happened. Here it is that our sensuality can save us *in extremis:* the atmosphere of the day that event took place, the way the trees and buildings looked, what we said to the person who was both the bearer and fellow recipient of that message and what that person replied, words that were not words but sounds out of time, taken out of any eternal context in which their content would be recognizable—these facts have entered our consciousness once and for all, have spread through us even into our pores like a marvelous antidote to the cup that the next moment had already prepared and which, whether hemlock or nectar, could only have proved fatal because it *was* the next, bringing with it the unspoken message that motion could be accomplished only in time, that is in a preordained succession of moments which must carry us far from here, far from this impassive but real moment of understanding which may be the only one we shall ever know, even if it is merely the first of an implied infinite series. But what if this were all? What if it were true that "once is enough"? That all consequences, all resonances of this singular event were to be cut off by virtue of its very singularity; nay, that even for memory, insofar as it can profit anyone, this instant were to be as though it had never existed, expunged from the chronicles of recorded time, fallen lower than the last circle of hell into a pit of total negation, and all this in our own best interests, so that we might not be led astray into imagining its goodness infinitely extendible, a thing that could never happen given the absolute and all-pervading nature of that goodness, destined to occur only once in the not-to-be-repeated cycle of eternity? Yet this seems not quite right, a little too pat perhaps, and here again it is our senses that are of some use to us in distinguishing verity from falsehood. For they never would have been able to capture the emanations from that special point of life if they were not meant to do something with them, weave them into the pattern of the days that come after, sunlit or plunged in shadow as they may be, but each with the identifying scarlet thread that runs through the whole warp and woof of the design, sometimes almost disappearing in its dark accretions, but at others emerging as the full inspiration of the plan of the whole, grandly organizing its repeated vibrations and imposing its stamp on these until the meaning of it all suddenly flashes out of the shimmering pools of scarlet like a vast and diaphanous though indestructible framework, not to be lost sight of again? And here we may say that even if the uniqueness were meant to last only the duration of its unique instant, which I don't for a moment believe, but let us assume so for the sake of argument—even if this were the case, its aura would still be meant to linger on in our days, informing us of and gently prodding us toward the right path, even though we might correctly consider ourselves shut off from the main source, never to be in a position to contemplate its rightness again, yet despite this able to consider its traces in the memory as a supreme good, as a god come down to earth to instruct us in the ways of the other kingdom, for he sees

that we have not progressed very far on our own—no far-
ther than those first few steps in the suddenly mild open
air. And we are lucky that he chooses so to deal with us,
for as of this moment our worries are over, we have only to
step forward to be in the right path, we are all walking in
it and we always have been, only we never knew it. The
end is still shrouded in mystery, but the mystery dimin-
ishes without exactly becoming clearer the more we ad-
vance, like a city whose plan begins to take shape on the
horizon as we approach it, yet that is not exactly the case
here because we certainly perceive no more of the divine
enigma as we progress, it is just that its mystery lessens and
comes to seem, whenever we stop to think of it which is not
very often, the least important feature of the whole. What
does matter is our growing sense of certainty, whether de-
duced by the intellect or the sensual intelligence (this is
immaterial): it is there, and this is all we need bother
about, just as there is no need to examine a man's ancestry
or antecedents in evaluating his personal qualities. But,
after the question of how did it get there, which we now
perceive to be futile, another question remains: how are
we to use it? Not only by what means, which is an impor-
tant enough consideration, but toward what end? Toward
our own betterment and by extension that of the world
around us or conversely toward the improvement of the
world, which we might believe would incidentally render
us as its citizens better people, even though this were just a
side effect? The answer is in our morning waking. For just
as we begin our lives as mere babes with the imprint of
nothing in our heads, except lingering traces of a previous
existence which grow fainter and fainter as we progress

until we have forgotten them entirely, only by this time
other notions have imposed themselves so that our infant
minds are never a complete *tabula rasa,* but there is always
something fading out or just coming into focus, and this
whatever-it-is is always projecting itself on us, escalating
its troops, prying open the shut gates of our sensibility and
pouring in to augment its forces that have begun to take
over our naked consciousness and driving away those
shreds of another consciousness (although not, perhaps,
forever—nothing is permanent—but perhaps until our last
days when their forces shall again mass on the borders of
our field of perception to remind us of that other old exist-
ence which we are now called to rejoin) so that for a mo-
ment, between the fleeing and the pursuing armies there is
almost a moment of peace, of purity in which what we are
meant to perceive could almost take shape in the empty
air, if only there were time enough, and yet in the time it
takes to perceive the dimness of its outline we can if we are
quick enough seize the meaning of that assurance, before
returning to the business at hand—just, I say, as we begin
each day in this state of threatened blankness which is
wiped away so soon, but which leaves certain illegible
traces, like chalk dust on a blackboard after it has been
erased, so we must learn to recognize it as the form—the
only one—in which such fragments of the true learning as
we are destined to receive will be vouchsafed to us, if at all.
The unsatisfactoriness, the frowns and squinting, the itch-
ing and scratching as you listen without taking in what is
being said to you, or only in part, so that you cannot piece
the argument together, should not be dismissed as signs of
our chronic all-too-human weakness but welcomed and

examined as signs of life in which part of the whole truth
lies buried. And as the discourse continues and you think
you are not getting anything out of it, as you yawn and
rub your eyes and pick your nose or scratch your head, or
nudge your neighbor on the hard wooden bench, this
knowledge is getting through to you, and taking just the
forms it needs to impress itself upon you, the forms of your
inattention and incapacity or unwillingness to understand.
For it is certain that you will rise from the bench a new
person, and even before you have emerged into the full
daylight of the street you will feel that a change has begun
to operate in you, within your very fibers and sinews, and
when the light of the street floods over you it will have be-
come real at last, all traces of doubt will have been pulver-
ized by the influx of light slowly mounting to bury those
crass seamarks of egocentricity and warped self-esteem you
were able to navigate by but which you no longer need
now that the rudder has been swept out of your hands, and
this whole surface of daylight has become one with that
other remembered picture of light, when you were setting
out, and which you feared would disappear because of its
uniqueness, only now realizing that this singleness was the
other side of the coin of its many-faceted diversity and in-
terest, and that it may be simultaneously cherished for the
former and lived in thanks to the versatility of the latter. It
may be eaten, and breathed, and it would indeed have no
reason to exist if this were not the case. So I think that the
question of how we are going to use the reality of our reve-
lation, as well as to what end, has now been resolved. First
of all we see that these two aspects of our question are ac-
tually one and the same, that there is only one aspect as

well as only one question, that to wonder how is the same as beginning to know why. For no choice is possible. In the early moments of wondering after the revelation had been received it could have been that this way of doing seemed to promise more, that that one had already realized its potential, that therefore there was matter for hesitation and the possibility of loss between a way that had already proved itself and another, less sure one that could lead to greener pastures, to cloud-cuckoo land and even farther, just because the implied risk seemed to posit a greater virtue in the acceptance. But it is certain now that these two ways are the same, that we *have* them both, the risk and the security, merely through being human creatures subject to the vicissitudes of time, our earthly lot. So that this second kind of happiness is merely a fleshed-out, realized version of that ideal first kind, and more to be prized because its now ripe contours enfold both the promise and the shame of our human state, which they therefore proceed to transmute into something that is an amalgam of both, the faithful reflection of the idealistic concept that got us started along this path, but a reflection which is truer than the original because more suited to us, and whose shining perspectives we can feel and hold, clenching the journey to us like the bread and meat left by the wayside for the fatigued traveler by an anonymous Good Samaritan—ourselves, perhaps, just as Hop-o'-My-Thumb distributed crumbs along the way to guide him back in the dark, only these the birds have miraculously spared: they are ours. To know this is to be able to relax without any danger of becoming stagnant. Thus the difficulty of living with the unfolding of the year is erased, the preparing for

spring and then for the elusive peace of summer, followed
by the invigorating readjustments of autumn and the dif-
ficult and never very successful business of adapting to
winter and the approach of another year. This way we are
automatically attuned to these progressions and can forget
about them; what matters is us and not what time makes
of us, or rather it is what we make of ourselves that mat-
ters. What is this? Just the absorption of ourselves seen
from the outside, when it is really what is going on inside
us—all this overheard chatter and speculation and the
noises of the day as it wears on into the calm of night, joy-
ful or abysmal as it may be: this doesn't matter once we
have accepted it and taken it inside us to be the interior
walls of our chamber, the place where we live. And so all
these conflicting meaningless details arc transformed into
something peaceful that surrounds, like wallpaper that
could be decorated with scenes of shipwrecks or military
attributes or yawning crevasses in the earth and which
doesn't matter, which indeed can paradoxically heighten
the feeling of a peaceful domestic interior. Yet this space
wasn't made just for the uses of peace, but also for action,
for planned assaults on the iniquity and terror outside,
though this doesn't mean either that we shall have at some
point to go outside or on the contrary that our plans will
remain at the stage of dreams or armies in the fire: we
carry both inside and outside around with us as we move
purposefully toward an operation that is going to change
us on every level, and is also going to alter the balance of
power of happiness in the world in our favor and that of all
the human beings in the world. And how is this to become
possible? Let us assume for the sake of argument that the

blizzard I spoke of earlier has occurred, shattering the frail
décor of your happiness like a straw house, replunging you
and your world into the grey oblivion you had been floun-
dering in all your life until the day your happiness was
given to you as a gift, a reward or so it seemed for the stale
unprofitable journey you called your life, only now it
seemed that it was just beginning, and at the same mo-
ment you had an impression of stopping or ending. Appar-
ently then happiness was to be a fixed state, but then you
perceived that it was both fixed and mobile at the same
time, like a fixed source of light with rays running out
from and connecting back to it. This suited you very well,
because it replied to your twin urges to act and to remain
at peace with yourself and with the warring elements out-
side. And now these have again taken over and crushed
your fragile dream of happiness, so that it all seems mean-
ingless. Gazing out at the distraught but inanimate world
you feel that you have lapsed back into the normal way
things are, that what you were feeling just now was a nov-
elty and hence destined to disappear quickly, its sole pur-
pose if any being to light up the gloom around you suf-
ficiently for you to become aware of its awesome extent,
more than the eye and the mind can take in. The tempta-
tion here is to resume the stoic pose, tinged with irony and
self-mockery, of times before. There was no point in arriv-
ing at this place, but neither, you suppose, would there
have been any in avoiding it. It is all the same to you. And
you turn away from the window almost with a sense of re-
lief, to bury yourself again in the task of sorting out the
jumbled scrap basket of your recent days, without any
hope of completing it or even caring whether it gets done

or not. But you find that you are unable to pick up the threads where you left off; the details of things shift and their edges swim before your tired eyes; it is impossible to make even the rudimentary sense of them that you once could. You see that you cannot do without it, that singular isolated moment that has now already slipped so far into the past that it seems a mere spark. You cannot do without it and you cannot have it. At this point a drowsiness overtakes you as of total fatigue and indifference; in this unnatural, dreamy state the objects you have been contemplating take on a life of their own, in and for themselves. It seems to you that you are eavesdropping and can understand their private language. They are not talking about you at all, but are telling each other curious private stories about things you can only half comprehend, and other things that have a meaning only for themselves and are beyond any kind of understanding. And these in turn would know other sets of objects, limited to their own perceptions and at the limit of the scope of visibility of those that discuss them and dream about them. It could be that time and space are filled up with these to infinity and beyond; that there is no such thing as a void, only endless lists of things that may or may not be aware of one another, the "sad variety of woe." And this pointless diversity plunges you into a numbing despair and blankness. The whole world seems dyed the same melancholy hue. Nothing in it can arouse your feelings. Even the sun seems dead. And all because you succumbed to what seemed an innocent and perfectly natural craving, to have your cake and eat it too, forgetting that, widespread as it is, it cannot be excused on any human grounds because it cannot be re-

alized. Therefore even to contemplate it is a sin. But, you
say, in those first moments . . . Never mind that now. You
must forget them. The dream that was fleetingly revealed
to you was a paradox, and for this reason must be forgot-
ten as quickly as possible. But, you continue to argue, it
mattered precisely because it was a paradox and about to
be realized here on earth, in human terms; otherwise one
would have forgotten it as quickly as any morning dream
that clings to you in the first few waking moments, until its
incongruities become blatant in the reasonable daylight
that seeps back into your consciousness. It was not a case
of a spoiled child asking its mother for something for the
nth time or of wishing on a star; it was a *new arrangement*
that existed and was on the point of working. And now it is
all the same; any miracles, if there ever are any again, will
be partial ones, mere virtuosic exhibitions beside the in-
controvertible reality of that other, as amazingly real as a
new element or a new dimension. And so it goes. But if it
was indeed as real as all that, then it *was* real, and there-
fore it *is* real. Just as matter cannot be added to or sub-
tracted from the universe, or energy destroyed, so with
something real, that is, real in the sense you understood it
and understand it. When will you realize that your dreams
have eternal life? I of course don't mean that you are a
moonstruck dreamer, but that they do exist, outside of you,
without your having to do anything about it. Even if you
do something it won't matter. And it is possible that you
will always remain unaware of their existence; this won't
matter either, to them, that is. But you must try to seize
the truth of this: whatever was, is, and must be. The dark-
ness that surrounds you now does not exist, because it

never had any independent existence: you created it out of the spleen and torment you felt. It looks real enough to hide you from the light of the sun, but its reality is as specious as that of a mirage. The clouds are dispersing. And nothing comes to take their place, to interpose itself between you and the reality which you dreamed and which is therefore real. This new arrangement is already guiding your steps and indicating the direction you should take without your realizing it, for it is invisible now; it still seems that it is lost for there is of course no tangible evidence of it: *that* happens only once, it is true. But now to have absorbed the lesson, to have recovered from the shock of not being able to remember it, to again be setting out from the beginning—is this not something good to you? You no longer have to remember the principles, they seem to come to you like fragments of a buried language you once knew. You are like the prince in the fairy tale before whom the impenetrable forest opened and then the gates of the castle, without his knowing why. The one thing you want is to pause so as to puzzle all this out, but that is impossible; you are moving much too quickly for your momentum to be halted. How will it all turn out? What will the end be? But these are questions of the ignorant novice which you have forgotten about already. You think now only in terms of the speed with which you advance, and which you drink in like oxygen; it has become the element in which you live and which is you. Nothing else matters.

And so, not bothering about anything, you again took things into your own hands. You were a little incredulous as to the outcome, but you decided to try it anyway. Who could tell what would happen? It didn't do to dwell too much on those ideal forms of happiness that had haunted you ever since the cradle and had now defined themselves almost in a paroxysm; they could be assigned to the corners and cubbyholes of your mind since it didn't matter whether they were in evidence as long as you never actually lost sight of them. What did matter now was getting down to business, or back to the business of day-to-day living with all the tiresome mechanical problems that this implies. And it was just here that philosophy broke down completely and was of no use. How to deal with the new situations that arise each day in bunches or clusters, and which resist categorization to the point where any rational attempt to deal with them is doomed from the start? And in particular how to deal with this one that faces you now, which has probably been with you always; now it has a different name and a different curriculum vitae; its qualities are combined in such a way as to seem different from all that has gone before, but actually it is the same old surprise that you have always lived with. Forget about the details of name and place, forget also the concepts and archetypes that haunt you and which are as much a part of the typical earthbound situation you find yourself in as those others: neither the concept nor the state of affairs logically deduced from it is going to be of much help to you now. What is required is the ability to enter into the complexities of the situation as though it really weren't

new at all, which it isn't, as one takes the first few steps
into a labyrinth. Here one abruptly finds one's intuition
tailored to the needs of the new demanding syndrome;
each test is passed flawlessly, as though in a dream, and
the complex climate that is formed by the vacillating wills
and energies of the many who surround you becomes as
easy as pie for you. You take on all comers but you do not
advertise your presence. Right now it is important to slip
as quickly as possible into the Gordian contours of the
dank, barren morass (or so it seems at present) without ut-
tering so much as a syllable; to live in that labyrinth that
seems to be directing your steps but in reality it is you who
are creating its pattern, embarked on a new, fantastically
difficult tactic whose success is nevertheless guaranteed.
You know this. But it will be a long time before the ordi-
nary assurances will be able to make themselves felt in the
strange, closed-off state you are in now. You may as well
forget them and abandon yourself to the secret grow-
ing that has taken over. Nothing can stop it, so there
is no point in worrying about it or even thinking about it.

How we move around in our little ventilated situation,
how roomy it seems! There is so much to do after all, so
many people to be with, and we like them all. But mean-
while it seems as if our little space were moving counter to
us, dragging us backward. We have reached this far point
of where we are by following someone's advice, and at
times it seems as though it might have been the wrong ad-
vice. If this were the case, to become aware of it would be
no help because we have refined the baser elements out of

our present situation and are technically on the same footing with others of different origins who meet and socialize with us. One sign of this is that no one remarks on the lateness of the hour, for we all believe we have reached a point where such details no longer count; we believe that we are immune to time because we are "out of" it. Yet we know dimly that the stillness we have attained is racing forward faster than ever toward its rendezvous with the encroaching past; we know this and we turn from it, to take refuge in dreams where all is not exactly well either, in which we reach the summit of our aspirations to find the mass below riddled and honeycombed with vacancy, yet there is room on the crest to move around in; it might almost qualify as an oasis. But as we all know, the thing about an oasis is that the whole desert has to become one before its exotic theories can benefit us, and even that would not be enough because then there would be too much of a contrast with the ordinary temperate climate leading up to it. Yet one can very well live and enjoy the fruits of one's considerable labors in arriving at this place which could be the end of the world in no unfavorable sense; there are the same things to look at and be surrounded by although in lesser numbers; what it is is quality as opposed to quantity. But can the one exist without the other? These thoughts oppress one in the social world one has built around oneself, especially the thought of these other infinite worlds upon worlds; and when one really examines one's own world in the harsher light of its happiness-potential one sees that it is a shambles indeed. Yet there is air to breathe. One may at least stay here a while hoping for more and better things to come.

That's the way it goes. For many weeks you have been ex-
ploring what seemed to be a profitable way of doing. You
discovered that there was a fork in the road, so first you
followed what seemed to be the less promising, or at any
rate the more obvious, of the two branches until you felt
you had a good idea of where it led. Then you returned to
investigate the more tangled way, and for a time its intri-
cacies seemed to promise a more complex and therefore a
more practical goal for you, one that could be picked up in
any number of ways so that all its faces or applications
could be thoroughly scrutinized. And in so doing you
began to realize that the two branches were joined to-
gether again, farther ahead; that this place of joining was
indeed the end, and that it was the very place you set out
from, whose intolerable mixture of reality and fantasy had
started you on the road which has now come full circle. It
has been an absorbing puzzle, but in the end all the pieces
fit together like a ghost story that turns out to have a per-
fectly rational explanation. Nothing remains but to begin
living with this discovery, that is, without the hope men-
tioned above. Even this is not so easy, for the reduced
mode or scope must itself be nourished by a form of hope,
or hope that doesn't take itself seriously. One must move
very fast in order to stay in the same place, as the Red
Queen said, the reason being that once you have decided
there is no alternative to remaining motionless you must
still learn to cope with the onrushing tide of time and all
the confusing phenomena it bears in its wake, some of
which perfectly resemble the unfinished but seemingly sal-

vageable states of reality at cross-purposes with itself that
first caused you to grow restless, to begin fidgeting with
various impractical schemes that were in the end, we have
seen, finally reduced to zero. Yet they cannot be banished
from the system any more than physical matter can, and
their nature, which is part and parcel of their existence, is
to remain incomplete, clamoring for wholeness. So that
now two quite other and grimmer alternatives present
themselves: that of staying where you are and risking
eventual destruction at the hands of those dishonest coun-
selors of many aspects, or of being swept back by them into
a past drenched in nostalgia whose sweetness burns like
gall. And it is a choice that we have to make.

As a lost dog on the edge of a sidewalk timidly approaches
first one passerby and then another, uncertain of what to
ask for, taking a few embarrassed steps in one direction
and then suddenly veering to another before being able to
ascertain what reception his mute entreaty might have
met with, lost, puzzled, ashamed, ready to slink back into
his inner confusion at the first brush with the outside
world, so your aspirations, my soul, on this busy thorough-
fare that is the great highway of life. What do you think to
gain from merely standing there looking worried, while
the tide of humanity sweeps ever onward, toward some
goal it gives every sign of being as intimately acquainted
with as you are with the sharp-edged problems that beset
you from every angle? Do you really think that if you suc-
ceed in looking pathetic enough some kindly stranger will
stop to ask your name and address and then steer you

safely to your very door? No, I do not think you are
afflicted with that kind of presumption, and yet your pitia-
ble waif's stance, that inquiring look that darts uneasily
from side to side as though to ward off a blow—these do
not argue in your favor, even though we both know you to
be a strong upright character, far above such cheap at-
tempts to play on the emotions of others. And there is no
use trying to tell them that the touching melancholy of
your stare is the product not of self-pity but of a lucid at-
tempt to find out just where you stand in the fast-moving
stream of traffic that flows endlessly from horizon to hori-
zon like a dark river. *We* know that the pose you happen
to be striking for the world to see matters nothing to you, it
could just as easily be some other one, joyous-looking or
haughty and overbearing, or whatever. It is only that you
happened to be wearing this look as you arrived at the end
of your perusal of the way left open to you, and it "froze"
on you, just as your mother warned you it would when you
were little. And now it is the face you show to the world,
the face of expectancy, strange as it seems. Perhaps Childe
Roland wore such a look as he drew nearer to the Dark
Tower, every energy concentrated toward the encounter
with the King of Elfland, reasonably certain of the victori-
ous outcome, yet not so much as to erase the premature
lines of care from his pale and tear-stained face. Maybe it
is just that you don't want to outrage anyone, especially
now that the moment of your own encounter seems to be
getting closer. You can feel it in every pore, in the sudden
hush that falls over the din of the busy street and the un-
usual darkness in the sky even though no clouds are appar-
ent. Your miserable premature spring has finally turned

into the real thing, confirmed by the calendar, but what a
sad look it wears, especially after its promising beginnings
that now seem so far back in the past. The air is moist and
almost black, and sharp with the chill; the magnolia petals
flatten and fall off one after the other onto the half-frozen
mud of the ground where only a few spears of sickly green
grass have managed to lift their heads. All this comes as no
surprise, it is even somewhat of a relief, and better than the
dire sequel that those precocious moments seemed to
promise, cataclysms instead of the ominous hush that now
lies over everything. And who is to say whether or not this
silence isn't the very one you requested so as to be able to
speak? Perhaps it seems ominous only because it is concen-
trating so intensely on you and what you have to say.

"Whatever was, is, and must be"—these words occur
again to you now, though in a different register, trans-
posed from a major into a minor key. Yet they are the
same words as before. Their meaning is the same, only you
have changed: you are viewing it all from a different
angle, perhaps not more nor less accurate than the previ-
ous one, but in any case a necessary one no doubt for the
in-the-round effect to be achieved. We see it all now. The
thing that our actions have accomplished, and its results
for us. And it is no longer a nameless thing, but something
colorful and full of interest, a chronicle play of our lives,
with the last act still in the dim future, so that we can't tell
yet whether it is a comedy or a tragedy, all we know is that
it is crammed with action and the substance of life. Surely
all this living that has gone on that is ours is good in some

way, though we cannot tell why: we know only that our sympathy has deepened, quickened by the onrushing spectacle, to the point where we are like spectators swarming up onto the stage to be absorbed into the play, though always aware that this is an impossibility, and that the actors continue to recite their lines as if we weren't there. Yet in the end, we think, this may become possible; that is the time when audience and actor and writer and director all mingle joyously together as one, as the curtain descends a last time to separate them from the half-empty theater. When this happens—yet there is no point in looking to that either. The apotheosis never attracted you, only those few moments in the next-to-last act where everything suddenly becomes momentarily clear, to sink again into semi-obscurity before the final blaze which merely confirms the truth of what had been succinctly stated long before. But there does not seem to be any indication that this moment is approaching.

Except that the silence continues to focus on you. Who am I after all, you say despairingly once again, to have merited so much attention on the part of the universe; what does it think to get from me that it doesn't have already? I know too that my solipsistic approach is totally wrong-headed and foolish, that the universe isn't listening to me any more than the sea can be heard inside conch shells. But I'm just a mute observer—it isn't my fault that I can really notice how everything around me is waiting just for me to get up and say the word, whatever that is. And surely even the eyes of the beloved are fixed on you as

though wondering, "What is he going to do *this* time?"
And those eyes as well as the trees and skies that surround
you are full of apprehension, waiting for this word that
must come from you and that you have not in you. "What
am I going to say?" But as you continue gazing embarrass-
edly into the eyes of the beloved, talking about extraneous
matters, you become aware of an invisible web that con-
nects those eyes to you, and both of you to the atmosphere
of this room which is leading up to you after the vagaries
of the space outside. Suddenly you realize that you have
been talking for a long time without listening to yourself;
you must have said *it* a long way back without knowing it,
for everything in the room has fallen back into its familiar
place, only this time organized according to the invisible
guidelines that radiate out from both of you like the laws
that govern a kingdom. Now there is so much to talk about
that it seems neither of you will ever get done talking. And
the word that everything hinged on is buried back there;
by mutual consent neither of you examined it when it was
pronounced and rushed to its final resting place. It is doing
the organizing, the guidelines radiate from its control;
therefore it is good not to know what it is since its results
can be known so intimately, appreciated for what they
are; it is best then that the buried word remain buried for
we were intended to appreciate only its fruits and not the
secret principle activating them—to know this would be to
know too much. Meanwhile it is possible to know just
enough, and this is all we were supposed to know, toward
which we have been straining all our lives. We are to read
this in outward things: the spoons and greasy tables in this
room, the wooden shelves, the flyspecked ceiling merging

into gloom—good and happy things, nevertheless, that tell
us little of themselves and more about ourselves than we
had ever imagined it was possible to know. They have be-
come the fabric of life.

Until, accustomed to disappointments, you can let yourself
rule and be ruled by these strings or emanations that con-
nect everything together, you haven't fully exorcised the
demon of doubt that sets you in motion like a rocking
horse that cannot stop rocking. You may have scored a few
points there where you first took those few steps (no more
than three, in all likelihood) when you first realized the
enormity of the choice between two kinds of mutually ex-
clusive universal happiness. And you also realized the
error of forever ruminating on and repeating those fatal
steps, like a broken movie projector that keeps showing the
same strip of film—you realized this when you were al-
ready far from that experience which had indeed begun to
take on the unearthly weirdness of an old photograph. You
cried out in the desert and you collapsed into yourself, in-
different to the progress of the seasons and the planets in
their orbits, and you died for the first time. And now that
you have been raised from the tomb like Lazarus by ob-
scure miraculous forces you are surprised that the earth
isn't better than the one you left behind, that all things
haven't yet perfected themselves as you believe you have
done by dying and being resuscitated to the uncertain
glory of this day in early spring. You can't get over the fact
that conversations still sound the same, that clouds of un-
happiness still persist in the unseen mesh that draws

around everything, uniting it in a firm purpose as it causes each individual thing to bulge more brightly and more darkly at the same time, drawing out the nature of its real being. But that is the wonder of it: that you have returned not to the supernatural glow of heaven but to the ordinary daylight you knew so well before it passed from your view, and which continues to enrich you as it steeps you and your ageless chattels of mind, imagination, timid first love and quiet acceptance of experience in its revitalizing tide. And the miracle is not that you have returned—you always knew you would—but that things have remained the same. The day is not far advanced: it still half-seriously offers with one hand the promise that it pockets with the other, and it is still up to you to seize the occasion, jump into the fray, not be ruled by its cruel if only human whims. The person sitting opposite you who asked you a question is still waiting for the answer; he has not yet found your hesitation unusual, but it is up to you to grasp it with both hands, wrenching it from the web of connectives to rub off the grime that has obscured its brilliance so as to restore it to him, that pause which is the answer you have both been expecting. When it was new everybody could tell this, but years of inactivity and your own inattention have tarnished it beyond recognition. It needs a new voice to tell it, otherwise it will seem just another awkward pause in a conversation largely made up of similar ones, and will never be able to realize its potential as a catalyst, turning you both in on yourself and outward to that crystalline gaze that has been the backing of your days and nights for so long now. For the time being only you know it for what it is, but as you continue to hold on to it

others will begin to realize its true nature, until finally it
stands as the shortest distance between your aims and
those of the beloved, the only human ground that can nur-
ture your hopes and fears into the tree of life that is as big
as the universe and entirely fills it up with its positive idea
of growth and gaining control. So it is permissible to rest
here awhile in this pause you alone discovered: a little re-
pose can do no harm at this stage; meanwhile do not fear
that when you next speak the whole scene will come to life
again, as though triggered by invisible machines. There is
not much for you to do except wait in the anticipation of
your inevitable reply.

Inevitable, but so often postponed. Whole eras of history
have sprung up in the gaps left by these pauses, dynasties,
barbarian invasions and so on until the grass and shards
stage, and still the answer is temporarily delayed. During
these periods one thought enclosed everything like the blue
sky of history: that it really was this one and no other. As
long as this is the case everything else can take its course,
time can flow into eternity leaving a huge deltalike deposit
whose fan broadens and broadens and is my life, the time I
am taking; we get up in the morning and blow on some
half-dead coals, maybe for the last time; my hair is white
and straggly and I hardly recognize my face any more, yet
none of this matters so long as your reply twists it all to-
gether, the transparent axle of this particular chapter in
history. It seems that the blue of the sky is a little paler
each morning, as happens toward the end of each epoch,
yet one doesn't want to move hastily, but to continue at

this half-savage, half-pastoral existence, until one day the unmistakable dry but deep accent is heard:

"You waited too long. And now you are going to be re-warded by my attention. Make no mistake: it will proba-bly seem to you as though nothing has changed; nothing will show in the outward details of your life and each night you will creep tired and enraged into bed. Know however that I am listening. From now on the invisible bounty of my concern will be there to keep you company, and as you mature it will unlock more of the same space for you so that eventually all your territory will have become right-fully yours again."

I know now that I am no longer waiting, and that the pre-vious part of my life in which I thought I was waiting and therefore only half-alive was not waiting, although it was tinged with expectancy, but living under and into this reply which has suddenly caused everything in my world to take on new meaning. It is as though I had picked up a thread which I had merely mislaid but which for a long time seemed lost. And all because I am certain now, albeit for no very good reason, that it was this one and no other. The sadness that infected us as children and stayed on through adulthood has healed, and there can be no other way except this way of health we are taking, silent as it is. But it lets us look back on those other, seemingly spoiled days and re-evaluate them: actually they were too well-rounded, each bore its share of happiness and grief and finished its tale just as twilight was descending; those days are now an inseparable part of our story despite their air of immaturity and tentativeness; they have the freshness of early works which may be wrongly discarded later. Nor is today really any different: we are as childish as ever, it turns out, only perhaps a little better at disguising it, but we still want what we want when we want it and no power on earth is strong enough to deny it to us. But at least we see now that this is how things are, and so we have the sense to stop insisting every so often under the guise of some apparently unrelated activity, because we think we shall be better satisfied this way; underneath the discreet behavior the desire is as imperious as ever, but after so many postponements we now realize that a little delay won't hurt and we can relax in the assurance of eventual satisfaction. This was the message of that day in the street, when you first perceived that conventional happiness would not do for you and decided to opt for the erratic kind despite the dangers that its need for continual growth and expansion exposed it to. This started you on your way, although it often seemed as though your feet had struck roots into the ground and you were doomed to grow and decay like a tree. Nevertheless you were aware of moving, whether it was you who were moving or the landscape moving forward toward you, and you could remain patient with the idea of growth as long as the concept of uniqueness—that one and no other—shone like a star in the sky above you.

Today your wanderings have come full circle. Having

begun by rejecting the idea of oneness in favor of a plural-
ity of experiences, earthly and spiritual, in fact a plurality
of different lives that you lived out to your liking while
time proceeded at another, imperturbable rate, you gradu-
ally became aware that the very diversity of these experi-
ences was endangered by its own inner nature, for variety
implies parallelism, and all these highly individualistic
ways of thinking and doing were actually moving in the
same direction and constantly threatening to merge with
one another in a single one-way motion toward that invisi-
ble goal of concrete diversity. For just as all kinds of people
spring up on earth and imagine themselves very different
from each other though they are basically the same, so all
these ideas had arisen in the same head and were merely
aspects of a single organism: yourself, or perhaps your de-
sire to be different. So that now in order to avoid extinc-
tion it again became necessary to invoke the idea of one-
ness, only this time if possible on a higher plane, in order
for the similarities in your various lives to cancel each
other out and the differences to remain, but under the
aegis of singleness, separateness, so that each difference
might be taken as the type of all the others and yet remain
intrinsically itself, unlike anything in the world. Which
brings us to you and the scene in the little restaurant. You
are still there, far above me like the polestar and enclosing
me like the dome of the heavens; your singularity has be-
come oneness, that is your various traits and distinguishing
marks have flattened out into a cloudlike protective cov-
ering whose irregularities are all functions of its uniform-
ity, and which constitutes an arbitrary but definitive
boundary line between the new informal, almost haphaz-

ard way of life that is to be mine permanently and the monolithic samenesses of the world that exists to be shut out. For it has been measured once and for all. It would be wrong to look back at it, and luckily we are so constructed that the urge to do so can never waken in us. We are both alive and free.

If you could see a movie of yourself you would realize that this is true. Movies show us ourselves as we had not yet learned to recognize us—something in the nature of daily being or happening that quickly gets folded over into ancient history like yesterday's newspaper, but in so doing a new face has been revealed, a surface on which a new phrase may be written before it rejoins history, or it may remain blank and do so anyway: it doesn't matter because each thing is coming up in its time and receding into the past, and this is what we all expect and want. What does matter is what becomes of it once it has entered the past's sacred precincts; when, bending under the weight of an all-powerful nostalgia, its every contour is at last revealed for what it was, but this can be known only in the past. It isn't wrong to look at things in this way—how else could we live in the present knowing it was the present except in the context of the important things that have already happened? No, one must treasure each moment of the past, get the same thrill from it that one gets from watching each moment of an old movie. These windows on the past enable us to see enough to stay on an even keel in the razor's-edge present which is really a no-time, continually straying over the border into the positive past and the neg-

ative future whose movements alone define it. Unfortu-
nately we have to live in it. We are appalled at this. Be-
cause its no-time, no-space dimensions offer us no sign-
posts, nothing to be guided by. In this dimensionless area a
single step can be leagues or inches; the flame of a match
can seem like an explosion on the sun or it can make no
dent in the matte-grey, uniform night. The jolting and loss
of gravity produce a permanent condition of nausea, al-
ways buzzing faintly at the blurred edge where life is
hinged to the future and to the past. But only focus on the
past through the clear movie-theater dark and you are a
changed person, and can begin to live again. That is why
we, snatched from sudden freedom, are able to communi-
cate only through this celluloid vehicle that has immortal-
ized and given a definitive shape to our formless gestures;
we can live as though we had caught up with time and
avoid the sickness of the present, a shapeless blur as mean-
ingless as a carelessly exposed roll of film. There is hard-
ness and density now, and our story takes on the clear,
compact shape of the plot of a novel, with all its edges and
inner passages laid bare for the reader, to be resumed and
resumed over and over, that is taken up and put aside and
taken up again.

What place is there in the continuing story for all the ad-
ventures, the wayward pleasures, the medium-size experi-
ences that somehow don't fit in but which loom larger and
more interesting as they begin to retreat into the past?
There were so many things held back, kept back, because
they didn't fit into the plot or because their tone wasn't in

keeping with the whole. So many of these things have been discarded, and they now tower on the brink of the continuity, hemming it in like dark crags above a valley stream. One sometimes forgets that to be all one way may be preferable to eclectic diversity in the interests of verisimilitude, even for those of the opposite persuasion; the most powerful preachers are those persuaded in advance and their unalterable lessons are deeply moving just because of this rigidity, having none of the tepidness of the meandering stream of our narration with its well-chosen and typical episodes, which now seems to be trying to bury itself in the landscape. The rejected chapters have taken over. For a long time it was as though only the most patient scholar or the recording angel himself would ever interest himself in them. Now it seems as though that angel had begun to dominate the whole story: he who was supposed only to copy it all down has joined forces with the misshapen, misfit pieces that were never meant to go into it but at best to stay on the sidelines so as to point up how everything else belonged together, and the resulting mountain of data threatens us; one can almost hear the beginning of the lyric crash in which everything will be lost and pulverized, changed back into atoms ready to resume new combinations and shapes again, new wilder tendencies, as foreign to what we have carefully put in and kept out as a new chart of elements or another planet—unimaginable, in a word. And would you believe that this word could possibly be our salvation? For we are rescued by what we cannot imagine: it is what finally takes us up and shuts our story, replacing it among the millions of similar volumes that by no means menace its uniqueness but on the contrary sit-

uate it in the proper depth and perspective. At last we
have that rightness that is rightfully ours. But we do not
know what brought it about.

It could be anything, you say. But it could not have been
an exercise in defining the present when our position, our
very lives depend on those fixed loci of past and future that
leave no room for the nominal existence of anything else.
But it turns out you have been pursuing the discussion in a
leisurely way throughout January and February and now
to a point farther into the wilderness of this new year
which makes such a commotion and goes by so quickly.
These ample digressions of yours have carried you ahead
to a distant and seemingly remote place, and it is here that
you stop to give emphasis to all the way you have traveled
and to your present silence. And it is here that I am quite
ready to admit that I am alone, that the film I have been
watching all this time may be only a mirror, with all the
characters including that of the old aunt played by me in
different disguises. If you need a certain vitality you can
only supply it yourself, or there comes a point, anyway,
when no one's actions but your own seem dramatically
convincing and justifiable in the plot that the number of
your days concocts. I have been watching this film, there-
fore, and now I have seen enough; as I leave the theater I
am surprised to find that it is still daylight outside (the
darkness of the film as well as its specks of light were so in-
tense); I am forced to squint; in this way I gradually get
an idea of where I am. Only this world is not as light as
the other one; it is made grey with shadows like cobwebs

that deepen as the memory of the film begins to fade. This
is the way all movies are meant to end, but how is it possi-
ble to go on living just now except by plunging into the
middle of some other one that you have doubtless seen be-
fore? It seems truly impossible, but invariably at this point
we are walking together along a street in some well-known
city. The allegory is ended, its coils absorbed into the past,
and this afternoon is as wide as an ocean. It is the time we
have now, and all our wasted time sinks into the sea and is
swallowed up without a trace. The past is dust and ashes,
and this incommensurably wide way leads to the prag-
matic and kinetic future.

THE RECITAL

All right. The problem is that there is no new problem. It must awaken from the sleep of being part of some other, old problem, and by that time its new problematical existence will have already begun, carrying it forward into situations with which it cannot cope, since no one recognizes it and it does not even recognize itself yet, or know what it is. It is like the beginning of a beautiful day, with all the birds singing in the trees, reading their joy and excitement into its record as it progresses, and yet the progress of any day, good or bad, brings with it all kinds of difficulties that should have been foreseen but never are, so that it finally seems as though they are what stifles it, in the majesty of a sunset or merely in gradual dullness that gets dimmer and dimmer until it finally sinks into flat, sour darkness. Why is this? Because not one-tenth or even one one-hundredth of the ravishing possibilities the birds sing about at dawn could ever be realized in the course of a single day, no

matter how crammed with fortunate events it might turn
out to be. And this brings on inevitable reproaches, un-
merited of course, for we are all like children sulking be-
cause they cannot have the moon; and very soon the un-
reasonableness of these demands is forgotten and
overwhelmed in a wave of melancholy of which it is the
sole cause. Finally we know only that we are unhappy but
we cannot tell why. We forget that it is our own childish-
ness that is to blame.

That this is true is of course beyond argument. But we
ought to look into the nature of that childishness a little
more, try to figure out where it came from and how, if at
all, we can uproot it. And when we first start to examine it,
biased as we are, it seems as though we are not entirely to
blame. We have all or most of us had unhappy childhoods;
later on we tried to patch things up and as we entered the
years of adulthood it was a relief, for a while, that every-
thing was succeeding: we had finally left that long suffo-
cating tunnel and emerged into an open place. We could
not yet see very well due to the abrupt change from dark-
ness to daylight, but we were beginning to make out
things. We embarked on a series of adult relationships
from which the sting and malignancy of childhood were
absent, or so it seemed: no more hiding behind bushes to
get a secret glimpse of the others; no more unspeakable
rages of jealousy or the suffocation of unrequited and un-
realizable love. Or at least these things retreated into their
proper perspective as new things advanced into the fore-
ground: new feelings as yet too complex to be named or
closely inspected, but in which the breathless urgency of
those black-and-white situations of childhood happily

played no part. It became a delight to enumerate all the
things in the new world our maturity had opened up for
us, as inexhaustible in pleasures and fertile pursuits as
some more down-to-earth Eden, from which the utopian
joys as well as the torments of that older fantasy-world had
been banished by a more reasonable deity.

But as the days and years sped by it became apparent
that the naming of all the new things we now possessed
had become our chief occupation; that very little time for
the mere tasting and having of them was left over, and
that even these simple, tangible experiences were them-
selves subject to description and enumeration, or else they
too became fleeting and transient as the song of a bird that
is uttered only once and disappears into the backlog of
vague memories where it becomes as a dried, pressed
flower, a wistful parody of itself. Meanwhile all our ener-
gies are being absorbed by the task of trying to revive those
memories, make them real, as if to live again were the only
reality; and the overwhelming variety of the situations we
have to deal with begins to submerge our efforts. It be-
comes plain that we cannot interpret everything, we must
be selective, and so the tale we are telling begins little by
little to leave reality behind. It is no longer so much our
description of the way things happen to us as our private
song, sung in the wilderness, nor can we leave off singing,
for that would be to retreat to the death of childhood, to
the mere acceptance and dull living of all that is thrust
upon us, a living death in a word; we must register our ap-
praisal of the moving world that is around us, but our song
is leading us on now, farther and farther into that wilder-
ness and away from the shrouded but familiar forms that

were its first inspiration. On and on into the gathering
darkness—is there no remedy for this? It is as though a day
which had begun brilliantly in the blaze of a new sunrise
had become transfixed as a certain subtle change in the
light can cast a chill over your heart, or the sight of a dis-
tant thin ribbon of cirrus ebbing into space can alter ev-
erything you have been feeling, dropping you back years
and years into another world in which its fragile reminder
of inexorable change was also the law, as it is here today.
You know now the sorrow of continually doing something
that you cannot name, of producing automatically as an
apple tree produces apples this thing there is no name for.
And you continue to hum as you move forward, but your
heart is pounding.

All right. Then this new problem is the same one, and
that is the problem: that our apathy can always renew it-
self, drawing energy from the circumstances that fill our
lives, but emotional happiness blooms only once, like an
annual, leaving not even roots or foliage behind when its
flower withers and dies. We are forced to recognize that we
are still living in the same old state of affairs and that it
never really went away even when it seemed to. Well, but
what can we do about it? Because even though the hydra-
headed monster of apathy can grow a new head each day
to slash back at us with, more fearsome than the one we
just succeeded in cutting off, so too nothing says that we
aren't to fight back at it, using the sword that our condi-
tion of reasoning beings has placed in our hands. Although
the task seems hopeless and there is no end to the heads in
sight, we are within our rights in fighting back, the
weapon is ours to wield, and it is possible that by dint of

continually doing so we might at length gain a slight foot-
hold or edge, for the enemy's powers though superhuman
are not inexhaustible: we are basically certain that noth-
ing is except the capacity for struggle that unites us, foe to
foe, on the vast plain of life. We are like sparrows flutter-
ing and jabbering around a seemingly indifferent prowling
cat; we know that the cat is stronger and therefore we for-
get that we have wings, and too often we fall in with the
cat's plans for us, afraid and therefore unable to use the
wings that could have saved us by bearing us aloft if only
for a little distance, not the boundless leagues we had been
hoping for and insisting on, but enough to make a crucial
difference, the difference between life and death.

"It almost seems——" How often this locution has been
forced on us when we were merely trying to find words for
a more human expression of our difficulty, something
closer to home. And with this formula our effort flies off
again, having found no place to land. As though there
were something criminal in trying to understand a little
this uneasiness that is undermining our health, causing us
to think crazy thoughts and behave erratically. We can no
longer live our lives properly. Every good impulse is dis-
torted into something like its opposite; the people we see
are like parodies of reasonable human beings. There is no
spiritual model for our aspirations; no *vademecum* beckons
in the light around us. There is only the urge to get on
with it all. It is like the difference between someone who is
in love and someone who is merely "good in bed": there is
no vital remnant which would transform one's entire effort
into an image somewhat resembling oneself. Meanwhile
everything conspires to protect the business-as-usual atti-

tude of the diurnal scenery—no leaf or brick must be found out of place, no timbre ring false lest the sickening fakery of the whole wormy apparatus, the dry rot behind the correct façade suddenly become glaringly and universally apparent, its shame at last real for all to see. Appearances must be kept up at whatever cost until the Day of Judgment and afterward if possible.

We are trying with mortal hands to paint a landscape which would be a faithful reproduction of the exquisite and terrible scene that stretches around us. No longer is there any question of adjusting a better light on things, to show them ideally as they may never have existed, of taking them out from under the sun to place them in the clean light that meditation surrounds them with. Youth and happiness, the glory of first love—all are viewed naturally now, with all their blemishes and imperfections. Even the wonderful poetry of growing a little older and realizing the important role fantasy played in the *Sturm und Drang* of our earlier maturity is placed in its proper perspective, so as not to exaggerate the importance in the general pattern of living of the disabused intellect, whose nature it is to travel from illusion to reality and on to some seemingly superior vision, it being the quality of this ebbing and flowing motion rather than the relevance of any of its isolated component moments that infuses a life with its special character. Until, accustomed to disappointments, it seemed as though we had triumphed over the limitations of logic and blindfold passion alike; the masterpiece we were on the point of achieving was classic in the sense of the Greeks and simultaneously informed by a Romantic ardor minus the eccentricity, and this all-but-terminated

work was the reflection of the ideal shape of ourselves, as
we might have lived had we been gifted with foreknowl-
edge and also the ability to go back and retrace our steps.
And so, pleased with it and with ourselves, we stepped
back a few paces to get the proper focus.

Any reckoning of the sum total of the things we are is of
course doomed to failure from the start, that is if it intends
to present a true, wholly objective picture from which both
artifice and artfulness are banished: no art can exist with-
out at least traces of these, and there was never any ques-
tion but that this rendering was to be made in strict con-
formity with the rules of art—only in this way could it
approximate most closely the thing it was intended to
reflect and illuminate and which was its inspiration, by
achieving the rounded feeling almost of the forms of flesh
and the light of nature, and being thus equipped for the
maximum number of contingencies which, in its capacity
as an aid and tool for understanding, it must know how to
deal with. Perhaps this was where we made our mistake.
Perhaps no art, however gifted and well-intentioned, can
supply what we were demanding of it: not only the figured
representation of our days but the justification of them, the
reckoning and its application, so close to the reality being
lived that it vanishes suddenly in a thunderclap, with a
loud cry.

The days fly by; they do not cease. By night rain pelted
the dark planet; in the morning all was wreathed in false
smiles and admiration, but the daylight had gone out of
the day and it knew it. All the pine trees seemed to be
dying of a mysterious blight. There was no one to care.
The sky was still that nauseatingly cloying shade of blue,

with the thin ribbon of cirrus about to disappear and materialize over other, alien lands, far from here. If only, one thought, one had begun by having the courage of one's convictions instead of finishing this way, but "once burned, twice shy"; one proceeds along one's path murmuring idiotic formulas like this to give oneself courage, noticing too late that the landscape isn't making sense any more; it is not merely that you have misapplied certain precepts not meant for the situation in which you find yourself, which is always a new one that cannot be decoded with reference to an existing corpus of moral principles, but there is even a doubt as to our own existence. Why, after all, were we not destroyed in the conflagration of the moment our real and imaginary lives coincided, unless it was because we never had a separate existence beyond that of those two static and highly artificial concepts whose fusion was nevertheless the cause of death and destruction not only for ourselves but in the world around us? But perhaps the explanation lies precisely here: what we were witnessing was merely the reverse side of an event of cosmic beatitude for all except us, who were blind to it because it took place inside us. Meanwhile the shape of life has changed definitively for the better for everyone on the outside. They are bathed in the light of this tremendous surprise as in the light of a new sun from which only healing and not corrosive rays emanate; they comment on the miraculous change as people comment on the dazzling beauty of a day in early autumn, forgetting that for the blind man in their midst it is a day like any other, so that its beauty cannot be said to have universal validity but must remain fundamentally in doubt.

This single source of so much pleasure and pain is there-
fore a thing that one can never cease wondering upon. On
the one hand, such boundless happiness for so many; on
the other so much pain concentrated in the heart of one.
And it is true that each of us is this multitude as well as
that isolated individual; we experience the energy and
beauty of the others as a miraculous manna from heaven;
at the same time our eyes are turned inward to the dark-
ness and emptiness within. All records of how we came
here have been effaced, so there is no chance of working
backward to some more primitive human level: the spirit-
ual dichotomy exists once and for all time, like the mind of
creation, which has neither beginning nor end. And the
proof of this is that we cannot even imagine another way
of being. We are stuck here for eternity and we are not
even aware that we are stuck, so natural and even normal
does our quandary seem. The situation of Prometheus,
bound to the crags for endless ages and visited daily by an
eagle, must have seemed so to him. We were surprised
once, long ago; and now we can never be surprised again.

What is it for you then, the insistent now that baffles
and surrounds you in its loose-knit embrace that always
seems to be falling away and yet remains behind, stub-
bornly drawing you, the unwilling spectator who had
thought to stop only just for a moment, into the sphere of
its solemn and suddenly utterly vast activities, on a new
scale as it were, that you have neither the time nor the
wish to unravel? It always presents itself as the turning
point, the bridge leading from prudence to "a timorous ca-
pacity," in Wordsworth's phrase, but the bridge is a Bridge
of Sighs the next moment, leading back into the tired re-

gions from whence it sprang. It seems as though every day
is arranged this way. The movement is the majestic plod-
ding one of a boat crossing a harbor, certain of its goal and
upheld by its own dignity on the waves, a symbol of pa-
tient, fruitful activity, but the voyage always ends in a new
key, although at the appointed place; a note has been
added that destroys the whole fabric and the sense of the
old as it was intended. The day ends in the darkness of
sleep.

Therefore since today, a day that is really quite cool de-
spite the deceptive appearance of the sunlight on things, is
to really be the point when everything changes for better
or for worse, it might be good to examine it, see how far it
goes, since the far reaches of sleep are to be delayed in-
definitely. It is not even a question of them any more.
What matters is how you are going to figure your way out
of this new problem which has again come home to roost.
Will the answer be another delay, prolonged beyond the
end of time, and disguised once again as an active life in-
telligently pursued? Or is it to be a definite break with the
past—either the no of death shutting you up in a small
cell-like space or a yes whose vibrations you cannot even
begin to qualify or imagine?

As I thought about these things dusk began to invade
my room. Soon the outlines of things began to grow
blurred and I continued to think along well-rehearsed
lines like something out of the past. Was there really noth-
ing new under the sun? Or was this novelty—the ability to
take up these tattered enigmas again and play with them
until something like a solution emerged from them, only to
grow dim at once and fade like an ignis fatuus, a specter

mocking the very reality it had so convincingly assumed? No, but this time something real did seem to be left over— some more solid remnant of the light as the shadows continued to pile up. At first it seemed to be made merely of bits and pieces of the old, haggard situations, rearranged perhaps to give a wan impersonation of modernity and fecundity. Then it became apparent that certain new elements had been incorporated, though perhaps not enough of them to change matters very much. Finally—these proportions remaining the same—something like a different light began to dawn, to make itself felt: just as the first glimmers of day are often mistaken for a "false dawn," and one waits a long time to see whether they will go away before gradually becoming convinced of their authority, even after it has been obvious for some time, so these tremors slowly took on the solidity, the robustness of an object. And by that time everything else had gone away, or retreated so far into the sidelines that one was no longer conscious of those ephemera that had once seemed the very structure, the beams and girders defining the limits of the ambiguous situation one had come to know and even to tolerate, if not to love.

The point was the synthesis of very simple elements in a new and strong, as opposed to old and weak, relation to one another. Why hadn't this been possible in the earlier days of experimentation, of bleak, barren living that didn't seem to be leading anywhere and it couldn't have mattered less? Probably because not enough of what made it up had taken on that look of worn familiarity, like pebbles polished over and over again by the sea, that made it possible for the old to blend inconspicuously with the new in a union too subtle to cause any comment that would have shattered its purpose forever. But already it was hard to distinguish the new elements from the old, so calculated and easygoing was the fusion, the partnership that was the only element now, and which was even now fading rapidly from memory, so perfect was its assimilation by the by-standers and décor that in other times would have filled up the view, and that now were becoming as transparent as the substance that was giving them back to life.

A vast wetness as of sea and air combined, a single smooth, anonymous matrix without surface or depth was the product of these new changes. It no longer mattered very much whether prayers were answered with concrete events or the oracle gave a convincing reply, for there was no longer anyone to care in the old sense of caring. There were new people watching and waiting, conjugating in this way the distance and emptiness, transforming the scarcely noticeable bleakness into something both intimate and noble. The performance had ended, the audience streamed out; the applause still echoed in the empty hall. But the idea of the spectacle as something to be acted out and absorbed still hung in the air long after the last spec-tator had gone home to sleep.

JOHN ASHBERY, born in Rochester, New York, in 1927, is Distinguished Professor at the City University of New York's Brooklyn College campus, where he teaches creative writing. His 1975 volume, *Self-Portrait in a Convex Mirror,* won the Pulitzer Prize, the National Book Award, and the National Book Critics Circle Award. His most recent publications are a collection of his poems entitled *April Galleons* (Viking 1987), and a volume of his art criticism, *Reported Sightings: Art Chronicles 1957-87* (Knopf 1989). He is a member of the American Academy and Institute of Arts and Letters and the National Academy of Arts and Sciences. Twice named a Guggenheim Fellow, he was awarded the annual fellowship of the Academy of American Poets in 1982 and received Yale's Bollingen Prize in 1984. In 1985 he received a MacArthur Prize Fellowship and the Lenore Marshall/Nation Poetry Prize. He lives in New York City.